By God's Grace: VSO in Ghana

by

Barbara M. Challenger

Herdwick Books

By God's Grace:
VSO in Ghana
by
Barbara M. Challenger

Copyright Barbara M. Challenger
2015

The right of Barbara M. Challenger to be identified as the author of this Work has been asserted by her in accordance with the Copyright, Designs and Patents Act 1988.

All rights reserved. No part of this publication may be reproduced, transmitted, or stored in a retrieval system, in any form or by any means, without permission in writing from the author.

ISBN 978-0-9571476-3-8

Ghanaian Adinkra Symbol GYE NYAME
'except for God'

Symbol of the supremacy of God.

For Moy

Contents

Ghanaian Adinkra Symbol GYE NYAME 'except for God' 3
Introduction 11
Context 12
In-country training (ICT) 14
Returning to the UK 22
First weekend in Roman Ridge: A trip to Jamestown 33
My remit in Ghana 36
My first day in work 50
Independence Day 56
The black ink incident 61
Visit to the Katapor Schools, March 1st 2012 63
Accra Mall 74
Living in Roman Ridge: Marching and the bats 81
Other interesting features of the flat in Roman Ridge 90
VSO flatmates 94
Madge, Spot, Brownie and Fatty 98
Mungo: How the other half live 105
Pink chickens 109
The eyebrow incident 110
Osu: The Oxford Street of Accra 113
Visit to Koforidua 116
The Adabraka incident 121
Visit to Akosombo Dam and Lake Volta, 26th May 2012 129
'One Day' – a poem for my Ghanaian friend Kwame 135
Visit to the hospital 138

Trip to the Wii Falls and the Monkey Sanctuary
in the Volta Region 142

Trip to Lome, the capital of Togo 148

The tick incident 152

Ghanaian food 155

A trip to Makola Market, Accra 165

The Kayayo: A story with a happy ending 169

Some Ghanaian customs and other useful bits
of information 171

By God's Grace 185

Ghanaian children 190

Aburi Botanical Gardens 193

Single, white female 197

The proposal 199

African dance and drumming evening 202

Scottish country dancing in Accra 207

Accra art and craft centres 210

Alliance Francaise 214

Labardi Beach 217

The death of President John Atta Mills 220

Voting for a new president 222

Scare on a trotro 226

Visit to Elmina and Cape Coast Castle 227

Cape Coast Castle - a poem 232

Trip to a workshop in Tamale 234

Christmas and New Year 2012 236

Leaving Ghana 238

Return visit to Ghana, February 24th to March 24th 2014 241

Some dos and don'ts when you visit Ghana	245
Acknowledgements	255
Glossary	256
Useful Websites	260
Ghanaian Adinkra Symbol SANKOFA 'return and get it'	261

Introduction

I'd hear the phrase '*By God's Grace*' often during the time I spent in the deeply religious country of Ghana. Whether by His grace, fate or simply my destiny, the Republic of Ghana beckoned me. It's the country where I lived and worked for 12 months and had the most memorable year of my life. From nearly walking into a pair of mating black cobra to being moved to tears at Cape Coast Castle, there was rarely a dull moment.

It was often a challenge to keep cool mentally and physically whilst living and working in a different culture and tropical climate. Sometimes I had to just '*go with the flow*'. It proved to be a priceless experience I wouldn't have missed for the world.

Context

Located in West Africa along the Gulf of Guinea coast, The Republic of Ghana is about the size of the UK and has a population approaching 27 million. It shares a border with Burkina Faso to the north, Togo to the east, Côte d'Ivoire to the west and the Atlantic Ocean to the south. When it was a British colony, the country was more exotically known as the 'Gold Coast'. It became the first black nation in sub-Saharan Africa to achieve independence in 1957.

I flew to Ghana on February 12th 2012 from Manchester via Heathrow, arriving at Kotoka International Airport in the country's capital city of Accra. The flight was about 3,175 miles (airline) and took approximately seven hours. I went to take up a 12 month work placement. I'd be based in a Non-Government Organisation (NGO) called Ghana National Education Campaign Coalition (GNECC) which was located in East Legon, Accra. My placement had been arranged through Voluntary Service Overseas, or as the organisation's more commonly known, VSO. This was the second work placement VSO had arranged for me in a developing country as I'd worked in Nairobi, Kenya, for six months in 2010.

Since returning to the UK in March 2013, life hasn't felt quite the same.

There's simply a world of difference between living in and amongst the hustle and bustle of a capital city like Accra in a developing country, with its vibrancy, noise, chaos, colour, contrasts, street food, markets, trotros, craziness, frustrations and mass of people, and the small town of Bollington in Cheshire East which nestles within the so called 'Happy Valley' on the borders of the Peak District.

On my return to the UK, I re-joined a writing group which meets each week in the library in Bollington and started to compile a collection of stories about my time in the remarkable and never to be forgotten West African country of Ghana. As the number of those stories grew, they evolved into this book. I hope the stories provide a flavour of my life and experiences whilst I lived and worked in Accra and that you enjoy reading them as much as I've enjoyed reminiscing through writing them.

In-country training (ICT)

It had been touch and go as to whether or not I'd be able to take up my placement in Ghana in February 2012 as I'd fallen down the stairs in my house the previous December and injured my left shoulder. Although it felt as though I'd dislocated it, I was told that I had a rotator cuff injury and that this could be notoriously slow to mend. It proved to be the most excruciatingly painful and protracted injury I think I've ever had the misfortune to experience. The pain woke me up every night for months and I'd have to go down stairs to apply frozen peas until the pain eased sufficiently for me to fall off to sleep again.

I eventually got some physiotherapy on the NHS and was given some exercises to aid my recovery. I felt I had to let VSO know about the incident and the organisation was reluctant to allow me to go without a letter from the physiotherapist I saw confirming my fitness. I was told that there would be no medical facilities or treatment I could expect in Ghana.

Although the injury wasn't 100% cured, I managed to get a letter from the physio which stated that if I persisted with my exercises, it would continue to improve.

Maybe I was crazy. I wanted to go and VSO agreed.

I'd completed the pre-departure VSO training before my placement in Kenya and VSO decided I didn't need to do it again. This had included two weekends at Harborne Hall in the West Midlands where I, along with other prospective volunteers, completed various exercises, role plays, tasks, listened to health experts and returned volunteers and learnt about what to expect and how to keep happy, safe and healthy in our placements. The preparation was thorough, helpful and VSO's approach, professional. The organisation has had a lot of experience in that respect as the International Development Charity was founded in 1958 and has sent over 50,000 volunteers to over 140 developing countries since then. VSO's vision is of a *'world without poverty'* and has a mission to *'bring people together to fight poverty'*. Much of the training and preparation for volunteers is now done online.

I was also relieved, pre-departure, that all my immunisations were up to date from having been in Kenya and so I didn't need any more. That was a huge relief to me. Having a phobia about needles it was probably one of the biggest hurdles I had to overcome before my first VSO placement and I'm still not sure how I managed to get through them all. (They included jabs - or medication - for: Hepatitis A, Hepatitis B, Rabies, Cholera, Meningitis, Yellow Fever, Typhoid and Tetanus.)

I flew to Ghana with five other volunteers from the UK: Emma, Sarah, Leela, Nique and James. I sat next to Emma, a young, enthusiastic volunteer, on the flight from Manchester to Heathrow and we met the others at Heathrow. I'll never forget how excited Em was to be going to Ghana. I lost count of the number of times she told me. We were all to be placed with different organisations and would be in-country for varying amounts of time. The flight went smoothly enough in marked contrast to the frenzy of activity and apparent chaos that greeted us at Kotoka International Airport. I vividly remember one area in the airport where it seemed as though everyone from all the inbound flights had to pass, loaded down with luggage, and it felt like a mass of sheep with bags being herded into a pen with a narrow gate. It was a nightmare.

I always feel anxious going through customs at the best of times and in an unfamiliar airport this feeling was heightened. I found my heart pounding for no good reason.

There were long queues and staff were particularly keen to check our yellow fever vaccination certificates before we even got to the customs control. At the final hurdle our passport, visa and letter of appointment from VSO were checked. Everything did appear disorganised but maybe this was something we'd all have to get used to. Maybe this was part of Ghanaian culture. There appeared to be no clear systems but by following our noses, we all managed to get through.

Emerging on the outside of the airport building, the heat enveloped us.

VSO staff were waiting to collect me and my fellow volunteers. Samina, the VSO volunteer representative for Accra and who I would be sharing accommodation with, was the first person to greet me. She probably said 'Akwaaba', I can't remember, but I do remember she had a warm smile and was no doubt anxious to know who she'd be sharing with. We were all ferried to the Sun Lodge Hotel, where we'd spend our first week in Ghana. It was here we had our 'In-country training'.

VSO didn't actually provide the training as volunteers did the planning and training on the week long induction.

The purpose of ICT is clear. It's to give volunteers the opportunity to learn about the culture, politics and the country they're going to be working and living in and also get to know a bit of the local language.

My contingent arrived at the hotel around 1.00 am in the morning. Volunteers from other countries had arrived earlier and there were some volunteers who'd already been in Ghana for several weeks. They were attending the ICT as their small number hadn't warranted providing the training when they'd arrived. This made for an interesting mix of volunteers who'd been in their placements for a while and those of us who were completely new to the country. There were about 18 volunteers in total.

I remember trying to quietly open the door to my hotel room that I'd be sharing with Pegi, a woman from Canada. Why VSO hadn't put early arrivals to share with one another still eludes me but I do remember disturbing Pegi. She got up, gave me a big hug and welcomed me to Accra. That was so lovely of her and made me feel good. I've never forgotten her warmth and greeting. I do believe if it had been me, I'd have pretended to be asleep and waited for introductions the following morning.

Pegi was open, friendly, easy to share a room and get along with. She was one of the volunteers who'd already been in the country for a few weeks. She soon got to know about my 'injury' as I had to lie on the floor and do my shoulder exercises morning and night. There was a swimming pool at the hotel which was a lovely facility and I found that swimming really helped to improve my shoulder.

Sadly Pegi fell ill during our week long stay with a stomach bug. We'd been told that coconut juice was good for tummy upsets, but despite trying to locate some, I didn't manage to get her any. She spent time in our hotel room some evenings skyping her husband who she'd left behind in Canada. That was when she could get a broadband connection of course.

ICT went well although I personally didn't feel that the numerous ice breakers and 'energisers' we had to participate in were all necessary. They do seem to be the 'in thing' on courses but I found some of them quite tiring rather than energising! There were the usual 'ice breakers' where you share information about yourself with a group in one format or another. This is often done working in pairs where you tell a partner about yourself and your partner then reports back to the group. A particular ice breaker I remember on ICT involved all the volunteers standing in a circle. There must have been twenty two or more of us, including some of the trainers. In turn, each one of us had to give our name together with an animal beginning with the first letter of our name, (we had to do an imitation of the animal too!) followed by the name of the town where we would be based. The person next in the circle had to recount all the names, plus animals and the towns where the volunteers were based until everyone had provided this information. Whilst light hearted and fun, it was not without stress, particularly if you were number 20 plus in the circle, but I concede that the game did help you to remember people. Other energisers are used, as the term implies, to generate energy and wake you up, perhaps after a mid-morning break or after lunch. These might involve you chasing people around as part of a game or standing up doing various exercises or even singing, a bit like party games. I appreciate that they have a purpose, but I wasn't overly enthusiastic. Primary school teachers seemed to know and take the lead on most energisers. It did feel as though they were activities children would love.

In terms of VSO volunteer organisation, each major geographical area in Ghana (North, Central, East, West and Accra) had a volunteer representative. It was their job to liaise with VSO staff in Ghana on any matters of concern amongst volunteers in their area, to act as intermediary/spokespersons and to feedback to volunteers news and information from the VSO office. It was the VSO reps who delivered the ICT and Samina, my flatmate, was involved.

The induction process through ICT was useful and included a trip to the VSO office in Lebone and into downtown Accra to enable us to become familiar with catching trotros – the clapped-out, privately owned minibuses that are the most common form of public transport in Accra. Having been introduced to the VSO Ghana office, we went on to discover the Epo's spot (a bar) in Osu which was just about within walking distance. It was a cool spot in a popular area in Accra with a large screen TV on the first floor level. It was one of the first places where I took photos of my ICT group chilling in the balmy heat and enjoying ice cold drinks.

We also went as a group to Keneshie market and were in awe of the bustle, the volume of people, the colour and vibrancy of downtown Accra. On one evening, we were also taken to the Coconut Grove Hotel where salsa dancing was a regular Wednesday night event. In the Ghanaian heat, everyone was outside and at the Coconut Grove Hotel, the dancing was around a swimming pool which made for a fantastic setting. I couldn't get over just how many Ghanaian men were dancing and what brilliant dancers they all were. It was like watching a huge 'Strictly Come Dancing' performance.

Learning some of the local Ghanaian language was also interesting and useful and we were introduced through staying at the hotel, to Ghanaian food.

At the end of the week, all the volunteers who'd bonded throughout the stay, dispersed to the far reaches of Ghana to take up or resume their placements. Pegi was teaching in the north- west of Ghana in a town called Wa in the Upper West Region and had to leave very early in the morning.

I'd bought her some chocolate as a small parting gift, (we had a fridge so it didn't melt) and I'd intended to give it to her before she left. I was convinced she'd wake me up getting ready to leave. Unfortunately, I slept through her departure and never got the chance to say good-bye on the morning she left. We'd meet up again though.

Returning to the UK

When you return to the UK after living in a developing country it's a shock to the system in reverse. You view your surroundings, life and culture differently and it takes a while to adjust. That being said, I hadn't thought too long or hard about the impact that leaving Ghana would have and was having on me until I attended a 'Returned Volunteers' (RV) weekend which was held at Harborne Hall in Birmingham. These weekends are arranged by VSO to help volunteers adjust to coming back to the UK and to share their experiences. (For some reason, I didn't attend one on my return from Kenya, but decided to go post Ghana.)

I'd been back in the UK for about eight months. Up until then I'd kept most of the thoughts, feelings and emotions which my return generated to myself. I shouldn't have been surprised that I got emotional in one of the sessions at Harborne Hall. It enabled me to acknowledge what I'd experienced, what I was missing and simply to let go. It was also a relief to know that many of the thoughts and feelings I had were shared by other volunteers.

Despite my work placement coming to end, I'd stayed in Ghana for an extra month in February 2013 to avoid what I thought would be the worst of the UK winter weather. I had a return flight booked for March 14$^{th.}$ *'Don't rush back,'* was the shared message I received from most of my friends. The British economy, weather, and general depressive mood of the country were all cited as good reasons to stay in Ghana for as long as possible.

I wasn't prepared for my thoughts or mood when I touched down at Manchester airport to a snow covered landscape. I felt about as low as the temperature. I'd not worn a coat, cardigan, jumper or any item of clothing with sleeves for a year and didn't have a stitch on me to keep me warm. It was freezing and an hour long wait to be picked up at the airport didn't help. Standing outside the entrance to 'Arrivals' at Manchester airport, I felt in limbo. One minute I was in Ghana, the next I was standing with my bags, abandoned and forlorn. For a while it felt surreal and I just wanted to be back in the warmth of the country that had become familiar to me.

I couldn't believe the weather was so inhospitable in March. When I was eventually picked up and taken to my house in Bollington I found I couldn't get in. I'd left two sets of front door keys with different neighbours but the set I'd asked my next door neighbour to leave in the outhouse for me didn't fit. Baffled, but unable to resolve the key situation immediately, we drove on to Wakefield where I'd left my car in my mum's garage. I'd sort the house keys later.

We took what I call 'the scenic route' which meant driving from Bollington through the Peak District. We drove through Chapel en le Frith, Glossop and over the Woodhead pass, down into Holmfirth en route to Wakefield. We stopped at the top of Holme Moss to admire the views. It was here I took photos of a snowman and the snow covered landscape on my first day back in the UK to send to Awo (friend in Ghana) and her children. I knew they'd never seen snow before and would love the snowman.

It was good to see family and friends again and yet it also felt disorientating. Twelve months had passed and so much had happened but it felt as though time had stood still in the UK. I had so much I wanted to tell but soon realised that few people were interested in talking or listening for any length of time about the experiences I'd had and which now affected the way I was thinking and how I viewed the world. Maybe I had too much I wanted to talk about and didn't know quite where to start and what to focus on either.

My feelings about what felt like a lack of interest were mixed and ranged from surprise to disappointment, but ultimately I appreciated I just needed to accept the fact. I had to acknowledge that for most friends and family back in the UK, getting on with daily routines and enjoying life in the present is what matters most and whilst I knew they were happy to see and be with me again, that was sufficient. I was back and life goes on. I learned later that this experience was shared by many returned volunteers.

Before leaving Ghana, I'd booked to go on a four day retreat in Devon at the end of my first week back in the UK as I thought this might help with my transition. My thinking at the time was that it would provide a bridge between Ghana and home and give me some mental and physical space to assimilate the two. Whilst the beauty and tranquillity of the venue, the imposed silence (there was no talking whilst on the retreat) and intense programme of meditation and qi gong were all helpful at the time, I still had to come to terms with returning to the small town of Bollington where I lived. I had to re-establish my life in the UK and decide what I was going to do next.

The contrast between the environment and community where I lived in Accra (population estimated at 3,410,000 people) and that of Bollington (population approaching 8,000) was extreme.

In the community where I lived in Accra, in an area called Roman Ridge, everyone greeted me when I was out and about and being an 'obroni' (white person), I was instantly recognisable and, in one sense, a bit of a celebrity. In contrast, whilst I know many people in Bollington, there's a greater sense of anonymity. There is friendliness, but not the same openness and warmth that I experienced in the community where I lived in Accra.

I missed the warmth, colour and open, friendly manner of the people in the immediate community where I lived in Roman Ridge, but felt that maybe the heat and sunny climate contribute to the out-going nature of Ghanaians. I've also missed their inquisitiveness and the genuine interest they showed in me. Despite considering myself to be a fairly private person and leaning slightly, along a spectrum, toward the introverted, I can be more extrovert and as a result of my time in Ghana I've noticed that I feel and am more outgoing. I'm aware that I strike up conversations with strangers more readily and spontaneously than I used to, even though some people don't look as though they want to. It could well be the British weather that makes us more reserved, but most people are happy to communicate when you make the effort to engage with them. It just takes time and the will to do so. 'Connection' gives you a warm feeling inside. I'm also certainly much more prepared to haggle and barter in shops about prices, despite the strange looks I may get. 'Nothing ventured' applies to more of my outlook on life as a whole these days.

There are many things I value about returning to the UK though. I particularly appreciate driving my Mini again and being mobile. (I'm sure my feet are flatter and a size bigger due to all the walking I did in Accra.) It was and still is a pleasure to get in my car and drive around listening to the radio or music. I've stuck small English and Ghanaian flags on the inside front window of my car a la Ghanaian taxis. It reminds me of Ghana and continues to make me aware of how fortunate I now feel to be mobile and not reliant on trotros, taxis or my legs to get me from a to b. The flags were removed from the windscreen when I took my car in for its MOT, apparently because they were considered to be blocking my view. I beg to disagree and re-instated them immediately! I also appreciate clean running water from a tap, my automatic washing machine, hot baths and the constancy of the power supply in the UK -for the present at any rate! Thankfully, there have been no 'lights out' since my return. Power cuts were common in Ghana and did prove extremely irritating at times wherever you were.

Of the many simple pleasures I took for granted before going to Ghana, easy and constant access to fresh, clean water ranks highly as one of the ones I think about and now value most. Whenever I have a shower after working out at the gym or soak in a hot bath I think about how fortunate I am and how precious water is. I also reflect on how much we take it for granted. There is nothing nicer than feeling fresh and clean after having access to an unlimited supply of hot water and also drinking water straight from the tap. We are just so lucky.

I do appreciate living in my own house again and the comfort of my own bed together with all the memorabilia and paintings that surround me, but I have to admit I never really missed the 'things' I own and my possessions when I was living in Accra. I also appreciate the variety and quality of food available to me. This degree of choice has also proved a mental challenge. I struggle and at times feel overwhelmed by the vast amount and range of food and goods on display in our supermarkets and can find it hard to wander around without thinking about the levels of poverty and hunger which exist not only in Ghana but around the world. There were a few good supermarkets in Accra, but not with the huge variety of foodstuffs that we're accustomed to and certainly not at the low prices we pay for them. So many people in the community where I lived and throughout Ghana survive on basic starchy foods like banku or fufu (doughy, starch based accompaniments to a meal) and rice. They wouldn't even visit a supermarket. I've also felt anger and disbelief when I asked a woman who was reducing the price of bread and cakes at the end of a day in Marks and Spencer (M&S) what happened to the food which wasn't sold. She told me it was thrown away. I couldn't believe so much food was going to waste. I felt M&S should be prosecuted.

I miss the thud, thud, thud, thud which could be heard most evenings in my local community as families prepared their evening meals. This was the rhythmic noise of the huge (industrial size!) mortars and pestles pounding maize and cassava to make fufu. And although I've been out for lunch with friends and enjoyed wonderful food, there is nothing like sharing a meal from one plate with a friend and eating food with your hand as is customary in Ghana. It just feels good and creates a bond between you and the person you're eating with. Simply buying a cup of coffee in the UK throws up different thoughts now too: whilst I enjoy and do have a cup of coffee when I'm out and about, I consider the cost to be exorbitant. I convert the money for a latté into Ghana cedis and think about how much it would buy in Ghana. There are very few coffee shops in Accra and drinking coffee or tea is not something the majority of Ghanaians do.

Thinking of food and drink makes me realise how much I miss the street food that was so readily available everywhere in Accra and also the local spots. (A 'spot' is the equivalent of a pub in the UK but they are, for the most part, in the open air.) I particularly miss the local lager called 'Star' which I developed a thirst for. I'm not a beer or lager drinker here in the UK but it was great to order an ice cold Star in a spot when you were sweating in the Ghanaian heat, cool down, chill and take in the local scene by watching the Ghanaian world go by. Yep, an ice cold Star could really hit the spot. (Pardon the pun!)

I now have a habit, although I'm trying to curb it, of converting most of what I pay for in the UK (in addition to a latte) into Ghana cedis. To give you an example: I'm ashamed to admit that the cost of going to my hairdresser every month would probably be more than most Ghanaians would earn in a month; it's about the same as I received from VSO to live on each month too. I think twice about buying flowers and plants. On one level I know they're beautiful and I love flowers, but on another, they seem such a waste of money. Not surprising then that there are few florists in Accra. I only saw one florist during the whole year I spent in Ghana and that was when I visited Togo, although there was a shop in Roman Ridge shopping arcade near where I lived that sold house plants at incredibly high prices. It's arguably not a wise mind-set to adopt but living in a poor country does make you think and feel differently.

We are, on the whole, so very fortunate and tend, on the whole, not to appreciate this fact. It is all too easy to ignore or block out information or interest in what is happening around the world in poorer developing countries. War, famine, malnutrition, abuse, disease, extreme poverty are all harrowing issues. Much information is too sad and overwhelming to take on board. It's just too easy in the cocoons in which we thrive to carry on oblivious. I feel it has to be about balance though. As individuals, there is a limit to what we can do to really make a difference, but doing nothing shouldn't be an option either. Acting 'small, small' as the saying goes in Ghana, can make a difference and it would be good to appreciate and act upon this mantra accordingly.

Not having a work focus to return to is hard and I miss not working at GNECC. Although work and the work environment at GNECC were challenging at times, I'd become accustomed to the routines, patterns and processes of working for the organisation and missed all my colleagues at 'The White House'. It had taken time, but I felt established, appreciated and part of the team before I had to leave. I particularly missed sharing an office and talking with my colleague and friend Awo.

I miss everyone I knew in the community where I lived: Betty who used to sew for me; Nana who lived in a flat below and who had three lively children. I miss the children in the community who used to call out 'obroni' whenever they saw me. In particular I miss Romeo, his older brother Elvis and Dalali, one of the brightest little boys I've ever met and who adored playing football. We often kicked a football to and fro to one another in the area in front of the block of flats where I lived and behind the local shops where his mother worked. Despite my best efforts, I could never get them to call me by my name. There were so many beautiful children in

Ghana. I just miss Ghanaian people. They are warm, strong, colourful, generous and friendly. I also miss the volunteers who became my friends and who were there at the end of a call or text message, planned things to do every weekend and had so much energy. I guess I simply miss Ghana.

I believe everyone needs structure and purpose in life although we all find it in different ways. I now go to the gym regularly and so am keeping my body fit. I attend a philosophy group which helps develop my spirituality and the control of my mind and thought processes, in theory anyway. I appreciate that I'm able to spend time with my family and friends again. I particularly enjoy reminiscing, through writing stories, about my time in Ghana. I appreciate my writing group for listening and for giving me feedback on my writing. Despite these pleasures, I've yet to find my next challenge. I need a focus which will take me forward and enable me to do something I feel is worthwhile, purposeful and which will, in a small way, make a difference in this crazy, wonderful, unfair and unequal world in which we live.

PS: there are also things I don't miss about Ghana. Amongst these I would highlight: mosquitos, ants, dust, trotros, hand washing my own clothes, cold showers, sweat (excessive perspiration), hair loss (I think due to taking anti-malarial tablets and maybe different diet) and power cuts.

PPS: I never did find out how my next door neighbour came to leave me a set of keys which didn't fit my front door.

First weekend in Roman Ridge: A trip to Jamestown

It was my first weekend in the flat in Roman Ridge and another volunteer, Jo, was visiting us. She was based in a town called Asikuma in the Central Region which was over three hours from Accra on a trotro. For some reason I felt I wanted to see the Gulf of Guinea and the Ghanaian coastline and Jo offered to accompany me. It was my first trip anywhere in Accra on a trotro other than on the ICT week. Jo had only been to the city centre and coast before in the company of other volunteers who were based in Accra so she wasn't sure herself of the trotros we needed to take but we managed okay and finally reached Jamestown on the east coast of Accra. It's the oldest neighbourhood and port area in Accra and a major tourist attraction.

As is invariably the case when you're out and about in Accra, it was an experience. Being a keen amateur photographer, I wanted to take photos of everything and everyone that interested me. A ceremony was taking place in Jamestown on the Sunday we visited and, insensitively, I took a couple of photos as we passed by. A Ghanaian who was attending the ceremony walked up to me and challenged me aggressively about my camera and what I was doing. I thought he was going to snatch my camera and smash it. I apologised profusely but acknowledge, in hindsight, that I should have known better. Why would anyone want strangers/tourists taking photos of a personal family event, whether it be a wedding or a funeral? And on another level, culturally, many Ghanaians, particularly the older generation, still hold superstitions and myths about the use of modern technology, including cameras which take images of them. Some Ghanaians are also concerned about how images of them and their customs are portrayed and perceived in other countries. I was lucky to get away with my camera intact!

      Jamestown is a very poor but distinctive area in Accra where many of the inhabitants speak the local language of Ga. It was and still is a fishing community. The district is run down and the buildings old and dilapidated. It has great historical significance as many of the decaying structures reflect Accra's colonial past, including the Fort. Another landmark you can't fail to miss in Jamestown is the lighthouse. Built in the 1930s to replace the original one constructed by the British at James Fort in 1871, it's not a particularly remarkable or attractive sight but certainly stands out within the area. (It's about 30 metres high.) Apparently there's usually someone offering to take you to the top of the lighthouse for a small sum of money where you can catch some good views of the area.

      I remember walking across a large, open, red earth space with no obvious footpath before reaching the coast and the spot we were heading for to have a drink and something to eat. A group of young Ghanaian boys was playing football there. It was a scene I'd see many times. Boys and young men love to play football and any open, dusty space usually had some makeshift goalposts and was taken over by the game. I followed Jo along the edge of the make-do football pitch, keeping one eye on the football, and eventually we reached the spot which overlooked the sea. The powerful waves crashed wildly against the rocky coastline. The relentless pounding sent spray fizzling into the air with each wave creating a new pattern. The sounds of the battering waves and spray were mesmerising. The heady mix of bright blue sky, raging sea, rugged coastline and crashing waves, made it a spot from which you could sit and gaze for hours. We enjoyed a drink and something to eat and I felt happy to be by the sea.

We took a taxi back to the flat.

Safely in our apartment I reflected on the beauty of the ocean and on the poverty and decay I'd seen in the oldest parts of the city of Accra which reminded me a little of Havana in Cuba with its decaying beauty. I also thought about Ghanaian culture and how I'd acted inappropriately and unsympathetically, like an ignorant tourist trying to take photographs of a private function which I would not have intruded upon in my own country. It proved to be the first of many learning experiences in Ghana.

My remit in Ghana

The job title I took in Ghana was *'Policy Simplification and Communication Officer'*. I'd been provided with an outline of the areas where I was expected, at the time of receipt, to contribute but I was aware that these could change. In fact I knew from previous VSO placement experience that it was highly likely that they would. Flexibility is one of the key qualities which VSO feel volunteers should possess and I had learned from my placement in Kenya that it was necessary to tread carefully in a new organisation, and expect both change and a very different culture. You needed to feel your way into both the placement and the role. A gung-ho approach with the attitude 'I know everything I'm expected to do and can solve all your problems' was definitely not recommended or on my agenda.

The organisation I was working with was Ghana National Education Campaign Coalition (GNECC), *'a network of civil society organisations, professional groupings, educational /research institutions and other practitioners interested in promoting quality basic education for all',* to quote from the organisation's literature. Put simply, GNECC worked with individuals and groups who wanted to improve access to, and the quality of, early and primary education for children in Ghana.

The organisation had been formed in 1999, and had grown in membership to include over 200 organisations and individuals by the time I joined it in

2012. I followed another VSO volunteer who'd been placed in the organisation a year earlier. This hadn't been the case when I volunteered in Kenya where I was the first volunteer to be placed in the Government Education Department. This provided a new dimension to my placement as I assumed that in some way I'd be expected to build on the work my predecessor had started. This didn't happen quite as simply as that, but more on that later.

GNECC's small number of staff included: the GNECC National Co-ordinator; an Administrative Assistant, (who left whilst I was based at GNECC and wasn't replaced); two Programme Officers, one being my colleague and friend, Awo; one Research Officer; an Accountant; his assistant; the driver and a male guard who was replaced whilst I was at GNECC by a woman.

With a small staff and within financial constraints, the organisation worked on a number of projects and programmes but all with the same goal: *to advocate and put pressure on the Government to improve access to, and the quality of, basic education for all in Ghana.*

To do this, GNECC undertook a wide range of activities including research, partnering with other NGOs on education related projects, and playing a key role working with and pressing Government to develop and improve basic education policy and the delivery of it. In the past GNECC had successfully advocated and influenced Government policy to increase the amount of funding per pupil allocated to schools and to ensure stricter monitoring of the distribution of resources, including text books, to schools. The organisation was, therefore, working at a high and strategic level in Ghana. As well as the main office in Accra, GNECC also had the support of branches and other officers working in the ten regions of Ghana. (The ten regions include: Northern region, Upper West, Upper East, Volta, Ashanti, Western, Eastern, Central, Brong-Ahafo, and Greater Accra.) These 'local' branches could, in some ways, be considered the eyes and ears of the organisation 'in the field'.

At the forefront of GNECC's work was the overarching Millennium Development Goal (MDG) to ensure the global target of universal primary education for all was met by 2015. (See information on the MDGs at the end of this section.) To achieve this goal, another key area of focus was campaigning to enable access to education by special interest groups such as girls, children with disabilities and young people in difficult circumstances and especially those from disadvantaged communities. This was in line with the international Education for All (EFA) goals. (See information on EFA at the end of this section.) GNECC also undertook to track and monitor educational resources and the efficiency of service delivery. GNECC was legally registered as a charitable non-profit making body with a General Assembly (the highest decision making body) and an Executive Council (15 members responsible for the management of GNECC). Day to day management of the organisation was, however, delegated to a secretariat lead by the National Co-ordinator who was my line manager.

At the height of its power, which was probably a few years before I was there, GNECC was a strong force and voice in government, campaigning and influencing policy related to basic education in Ghana. During my placement, GNECC was actively engaged in the process of Organisational Development (OD) to improve its capacity and effectiveness.

I soon learned that I was not the only volunteer to be based at GNECC. The organisation was used to having a steady stream of young and more mature volunteers from Canada in particular. These placements were arranged through an organisation called World University Service of Canada or WUSC as it was known. Some younger volunteers were only placed at GNECC for short periods of about three months as part of their course of study at college or university. I got to know a few young Canadian volunteers quite well and one, Katie, better than the others as she shared the office where I was based. She was bright and confident and had good IT and statistical skills. She worked with the Research Officer on a project he was actively engaged in to stop violence against girls in schools or SVAGS.

WUSC also placed more mature volunteers with GNECC who stayed longer. Two were based at GNECC during my placement. Jules' placement was for a year and Waqas' was for nine months. They were tenuously called 'volunteers' as the conditions and terms under which they were based in Ghana were different and seemed quite generous, certainly compared to VSO. Jules had been seconded from a government position in Canada. He was tall, well built, sported a beard, had a calm, confident manner and very good people skills. He was with his wife who was working for another NGO in Accra. He'd previously worked in Malawi. Waqas was tall, slim, had jet black hair, a broad smile and was in my opinion, very handsome. He spoke a number of languages including Arabic and French and had worked abroad for the Government in Canada. He was well travelled, had an easy manner, was interested in people and travel and loved to talk. Jules focused on Organisational Development at GNECC whilst Waqas' role related to marketing. They were both friendly, supportive colleagues who I liked a lot, got on well with and respected. They shared office space with GNECC's researcher in the annexe to the White House. I remember Jules bringing sweets into the office which he kept in a small dish on his desk. He'd been sent jelly beans from Canada and generously shared them.

Waqas became my travel companion on a couple of occasions. (See later.)

As a result of staff shortage, I was unable to work directly with another member of staff to pass on and share skills although I shared an office with Awo who was the lead programme officer on girls' and women's issues. She was actively involved in a five year Partnership Project led by Action Aid, to promote girls' rights to education.

To begin with, the work and activities I was engaged in felt disparate and lacking in a common focus. I developed a work plan which was agreed with the National Co-ordinator. It was task orientated and included a number of specific pieces of work.

I wrote a simple version of the Government's long and complex plan to develop education in Ghana from 2010 to 2020. The plan was called the 'Education Strategic Plan' because it is like the umbrella plan under which all other plans and activities were developed and implemented.

All schools need to plan how they are going to improve the education they provide for their pupils. To help them to do this, I wrote guidance on how to produce what is called a 'School Performance Improvement Plan' or SPIP for short. This included what should go in the plan and who should be consulted during the planning process.

There are many problems in Ghana which are directly linked to the teaching profession. For example, there are not enough qualified teachers and it is difficult to get teachers to work in northern Ghana. I wrote a paper providing information on all the issues related to teachers and teaching in Ghana to help GNECC to bid to another agency to get money to look in more detail at these problems. Unfortunately, the bid was not submitted.

I also did a lot of research and wrote a paper on schemes and projects which have been used in different developing countries to help young children to learn to read. The project is called 'Early Grade Reading' (EGR).

I had a couple of other tasks related to documentation of GNECC activities and familiarisation with the VSO 'Tackling Education Needs Inclusively' project or TENI for short. TENI was a major VSO programme based in northern Ghana and was the main VSO project supported by Red Nose Day funding from the UK.

My initial work plan formed the basis of my activities for the first four or five months of my placement. I was undertaking research on the areas I was given and began to learn more about GNECC as an organisation and about the education system in Ghana and the many issues it was struggling with, such as the marked contrast between provision in the north and south of the country, the dire lack of resources, acute lack of qualified teachers and appalling school buildings and facilities to name but a few. It felt as though I was working independently for much of the time although I hoped that the outcomes would benefit the organisation and the achievement of its goals.

Working for GNECC was a new experience and a challenging one as I found the culture of the organisation to be quite different to my experiences of working in the UK although not totally different from my experience in Kenya. At times it felt frustrating and as if you weren't trusted, which may well have been the case as I was new, unknown and from another country. I also wondered to what extent this 'closed shop' approach was related to the fact that I was female – although from discussion with Jules and Waqas, I knew they experienced the same challenges and feelings. In this respect, communication was not as free flowing as I was used to when I worked in local government in the UK and meetings were infrequent.

It was hard to see how everyone could feel part of the organisation and fully involved when colleagues, including me, seemed to be in the dark about so many things. It was even difficult to find out where colleagues were if they weren't in the office. It felt like a 'closed' culture which I realised would not be changed quickly.

In the early days of my placement Awo invited me to join her in attending a programme/ workshop led by Action Aid in a local hotel which included officers from many different African countries. The focus of the project they were all involved in and of which the programme was a part, was supporting children's rights. I was fortunate to also go with Awo and this group of officers to visit two local schools within the Katapor community in Ga West (more on that later). I really appreciated this visit as my placement didn't include direct working in or with schools.

Just before leaving Ghana in August 2012 for a break back in the UK, I developed a project bid for funding from VSO, GNECC's partner, which provided me with a much more focused programme of work and activities. From September 2012 until the end of my placement the following February, I felt I was establishing a much clearer role and more coherent work plan within GNECC. This included producing a critique of the Government Special

Education Needs Department's draft policy on Inclusion and Special Educational Needs and presenting my analysis at a workshop arranged by the Government Special Needs Officers. I also developed a paper on the Ghanaian education policy development process, undertook a piece of independent research on key individual's and partners' perceptions of GNECC as an organisation and how it could improve its impact and produced a summary chart of the political history of educational development in the country.

During my placement I gave a presentation (ably enhanced, in relation to my slide presentation, by my flatmates Lizzie and Samina) on the importance of Early Grade Reading. This was delivered to the wider membership of GNECC. Although I was nervous about giving the presentation, the nerves soon dissipated as I was confident in my knowledge of the topic given the amount of research I'd done. I felt privileged to have been able to undertake the research and to share this. I also supported colleagues where I could during Global Action Week and at a number of workshops organised by GNECC. (See information on Global Action Week at the end of this section.) I was happy to support my GNECC colleagues in whatever way I could, feeling, as I did, that the goals of the organisation were so worthwhile. The work was interesting and rewarding and I enjoyed working as part of the GNECC team.

I learned so much by working at GNECC and, as with my placement in Kenya, felt I was fortunate to work with colleagues dedicated to improving educational opportunities for children.

In summary, I tried to give, share and support GNECC to the best of my ability, certainly gained much and hope that what I produced and how I worked benefitted the organisation and the wider education community in Ghana. I would find quantifying my impact, which is the focus of all VSO placements, more difficult. Measuring impact is not easy and requires agreement from the outset on clear, measurable targets and outcomes. Being able to objectively measure impact is a task which VSO continues to seek to improve upon in relation to its vision of alleviating poverty and its goal of ensuring the inclusion of all in education.

I was disappointed not to be able to extend my placement to complete the VSO project I had developed and for which GNECC received funding. For this I can only philosophically say *'c'est la vie'*.

Millennium Development Goals

The Millennium Development Goals (MDGs) are eight international development goals which were set out in 2000.

In September 2000, world leaders came together at the United Nations headquarters in New York to adopt the United Nations Millennium Declaration. This committed their nations to a new global partnership to reduce extreme poverty and set out 8 targets which have become known at the MDGs.

All 189 United Nations member states at the time (there are 193 currently), and at least 23 international organisations, committed to help achieve the following Millennium Development Goals by 2015:

1. To eradicate extreme poverty and hunger
2. To achieve universal primary education
3. To promote gender equality
4. To reduce child mortality
5. To improve maternal health
6. To combat HIV/AIDS, malaria, and other diseases
7. To ensure environmental sustainability
8. To develop a global partnership for development

Education for All (EFA)

The Education for All (EFA) movement is a global commitment to provide quality basic education for all children, youth and adults. At the World Education Forum in Dakar in 2000, 164 governments pledged to achieve EFA and identified six goals to be met by 2015. Governments, development agencies, civil society and the private sector are working together to reach the EFA goals.

Education for All Goals

Goal 1

Expanding and improving comprehensive early

childhood care and education, especially for the most vulnerable and disadvantaged children.

Goal 2

Ensuring that by 2015 all children, particularly girls, children in difficult circumstances and those belonging to ethnic minorities, have access to, and complete, free and compulsory primary education of good quality.

Goal 3

Ensuring that the learning needs of all young people and adults are met through equitable access to appropriate learning and life-skills programmes.

Goal 4

Achieving a 50 per cent improvement in levels of adult literacy by 2015, especially for women, and equitable access to basic and continuing education for all adults.

Goal 5

Eliminating gender disparities in primary and secondary education by 2005, and achieving gender equality in education by 2015, with a focus on ensuring girls' full and equal access to and achievement in basic education of good quality.

Goal 6

Improving all aspects of the quality of education and ensuring excellence of all so that recognized and measurable learning outcomes are achieved by all, especially in literacy, numeracy and essential life skills.

UNESCO (The United Nations Education, Scientific and Cultural Organisation) has been charged with leading the movement and coordinating the international efforts to reach EFA. Governments, development agencies, civil society, non-government organisations and the media are some of the partners working toward reaching these goals.

The EFA goals also contribute to the global pursuit of the eight MDGs, especially MDG 2 on universal primary education and MDG 3 on gender equality in education, by 2015.

UNESCO produces the annual Education for All Global Monitoring Report.

Global Partnership for Education (GPE)

The GPE is an international organisation launched in 2002 to focus on getting all children into school for a quality education in the world's poorest countries. GPE works with donors, developing countries, international organisations, foundations, the private sector, teacher organisations, and civil society organisations.

It was launched to accelerate progress towards the MDG of universal primary education by 2015.
GPE has grown from partnering with seven developing countries in 2002 to 59 in 2014. It is the fourth largest donor to basic education in low and middle-income countries.

Global Action Week (GAW)

Global Action Week is one of the major events in the education calendar. It provides every national and regional education campaign with an opportunity to highlight one area of the Education For All agenda.

During GAW targeted efforts are made to achieve change on the ground, with the added support of education campaigners and millions of members of the public worldwide joining together for the same cause.

My first day in work

Part 1: The journey

I'd been taken by a VSO driver to my workplace for a brief introductory meeting with my employer and so had 'done the route' once before. This initial workplace visit was chauffeur driven in a large, comfortable, air-conditioned VSO vehicle which had suspension. Even then the journey felt long and, of course unfamiliar, so I was under no illusion that my daily trip to work via the infamous trotros was going to prove a challenging and tiring one.

The building where I was to be based at GNECC was a large colonial looking house called 'The White House' for no more obvious reason than that it was painted white. The White House was near a landmark area called American House, which bore no resemblance to its name as American House was quite literally just a T junction with a number of street food sellers, a few shops and a stopping point for trotros. (I couldn't and still can't see any connection to American House although there must be one.)

During my first visit to The White House, GNECC's administrative assistant gave me instructions about how to get to work via trotros from where I lived in Roman Ridge. There appeared to be a number of options, but all of them, according to her, seemed to revolve around getting on a trotro from a bus stop at a place called Shangri-la and heading for Madina Market. I do remember wondering about the reliability of her information at the time though, given that she didn't actually use public transport herself.

So, on day one, I got up at 6.00am in order to reach my workplace in good time for my 8.00am start. I felt that this was too early a work start but thought I should make the effort to arrive on time on my first day in work at least. I caught a trotro very near to where I lived in Roman Ridge at around 6.40am on the first leg of my journey to get to the bus stop at Shangri-la. It took about ten minutes and I got off at the terminus for this trotro.

From the terminus for the first trotro, I had to cross a dual carriageway in order to catch the second trotro from the bus stop at Shangri-la. Although there was a pedestrian crossing with traffic lights, I soon learned that Ghanaians are totally unforgiving and intolerant drivers. They adopt the most aggressive approach towards pedestrians who never, under any circumstances, seem to have the right of way. This aspect of Ghanaian culture meant you needed to have your wits about you and considerable nerve in crossing any road, whether there were traffic lights or not. At the pedestrian crossing, the lights hovered on green (for pedestrians) for only a very brief period during which everyone who was waiting made a mad dash to span both sections of the carriageway before the lights switched back to red. It was always a huge relief to get to the other side in one piece. It felt as though you were a matador taunting the motorists as you dared to walk in front of them. As you invaded their space, they would be revving their engines waiting to charge at you if you were still in their path when the lights returned to green for them to go. Motorcyclists tended to ignore the lights completely, whatever colour they were.

Having survived the dual carriageway crossing in one piece, I followed the advice I'd been given and waited at Shangri-la to catch a trotro to Madina Market, intending to get off at 'The White House' which, I'd been told, the trotro would pass. That all sounded fine but as I've already said, I had some reservations beforehand about the instructions I'd been given and, as it happened, with just cause. What the administrative assistant had failed to tell me was that I needed to catch a trotro from Shangri-la which was going to American House and not Madina Market. In fact there were no trotros which passed the White House from the bus stop at Shangri-la.

So in total ignorance and in good faith, I caught a trotro to Madina Market and soon realised that the route we were going along bore no resemblance to that taken by the VSO driver on my initial visit. To add to this, I was being taken on the most tortuous journey around back streets and off the beaten dirt track roads filled with potholes. Realising I'd no idea where I was, and that the prospect of arriving in work by 8.00 am was fast slipping away, I resigned myself to the fact that I'd probably end up, at some time or other, at Madina Market.

I did ask the mate (the person who took the trotro fares) somewhat plaintively if he knew where the White House was but neither he, nor anyone else on the trotro, claimed to have heard of the place. Eventually, after my bones felt well and truly shaken, battered and bruised, I ended up at Madina Market. It was approaching 7.30am when I got out in the midst of all the hustle and bustle of an early morning market scene with no idea where to go to get to where I wanted to be. Fortunately, the mate on the trotro I'd just got off was helpful and started to ask other trotro drivers if they knew where the White House was. In my experience, the majority of Ghanaians really do bend over backwards to help you. We walked through the market to another trotro area, with me following behind the mate, where it seemed I could get on a trotro to American House. This was the landmark from which point I'd been advised I could walk to the White House. The trotro set off almost immediately, which was a bonus, but we had to wait for about ten minutes as we inched our way out of the log jam of trotros all competing to leave the market at the same time. It was chaotic but there was absolutely nothing I could do except 'go with the flow'.

To my surprise and relief, the trotro I caught from Medina Market actually passed the White House before carrying on to American House and I eventually got to work, believe it or not, just before 8.00am. The journey felt much longer and I was surprised to be the first person to arrive. I felt stressed, hot and bothered and prayed that subsequent journeys to work would prove more straightforward.

Part 2: In work

Being the first to arrive, I struck up a conversation with the guard who was posted at the gated entrance to the White House and checked out the journey with him. He explained that I simply needed to get a trotro that went to American House from Shangri-la as no trotros went past the White House from that bus stop.

So I learned, the hard way, that to get to work via public transport, my journey would subsequently consist of two trotro rides followed by a walk of about ten minutes from American House to the White House. Believe it or not, having been anxious about getting to work on time on day one, I had to wait around in the outdoor foyer area of the White House until 9.30am when the administrative assistant arrived to show me to the office where I'd be based. Ah well, this was Ghana and it provided me with time to cool off and down.

On a huge positive note, I discovered I could readily get internet access in work and was happy to make connections via email whilst I sat and waited for any colleagues to arrive. (I'd been advised by VSO that I would need to bring my own laptop for work purposes.) However, I was also to learn on day one that 'lights out', or power cuts, are frequent occurrences in Ghana. No sooner had I sorted out access to the internet on my laptop when the electricity went off which meant there was no Wi-Fi and, worse still, no air conditioning. As the morning wore on, I started to roast. It was boiling hot. My office was on the first floor with no air conditioning or fan and as time wore on, I could hardly keep my eyes open. I felt so hot, sticky and sweaty and just wanted to lie down and drift off to sleep.

As no-one else had arrived by lunchtime, I started to think about food. I'd been advised by another volunteer that there would be loads of places to get some 'chop' (the local name for food) so hadn't brought any with me. However, the nearest place to get something to eat was American House which was a good ten minute walk away. The downside to the relative proximity of American House was the fact that it was literally too hot at mid-day to walk anywhere as the sun was beating down and I had no hat or sun cream with me. A well prepared obroni…not! Added to that, my line manager had, by now, contacted his administrative assistant to say that he had 'an emergency' (although I never found out what it was), so wouldn't be coming into the office. In fact I didn't see my line manager or any other colleague there on my first day at all!

To summarise: my first day in work included the journey from hell, no food, being roasted alive in an office with no air conditioning and spending the day alone. It was a relief to leave at the end of the day. I walked to American House in the cooler part of late afternoon and bought some kelewele (spicy plantain) to eat on the trotro going home. My relief was palpable and the kelewele tasted great. I'd got through my first day in work which, as everyone knows who's started a new job, is the worst, but to start a new job in such a different country and culture and survive to tell the tale felt a major achievement.

The end of a not so perfect, but ever so memorable day.

Independence Day

March 6th is Independence Day in Ghana. It commemorates the country's freedom from UK rule which was secured in 1957. Ghana was the first black African country to gain independence so arguably this provides an even greater reason to mark such an important event. It's a public holiday and one Ghanaians, and non-Ghanaians alike, make the most of.

For me, Independence Day initially simply meant a day off work. I was grateful I didn't need to get up early to catch any trotros and then walk to work. It was definitely a day to celebrate and to rest and I was all for it. But even on the day, I was ignorant of how Ghanaians officially marked their independence other than by having a day off work. I'd heard there would be a formal event which included parades and marching by the military in Independence Square which I gathered was located near the coast. As I'd only arrived in Accra a week or so earlier, Independence Square was not a place I'd visited. I did know that the event would be broadcast on the television so my original intention was to catch it at my leisure in the flat as we were fortunate enough to have a TV. (It had been generously donated to a volunteer, now departed, by her employer and for which many subsequent volunteers were grateful.) Assuming there was electricity of course!

I hadn't realised how early the parades in Independence Square started, so by the time I got up the event was already in full swing. It was immediately clear to me what a huge scale event it was. All the top Ghanaian dignitaries, including the President, were there watching the parades and giving speeches from their elevated boxes. It was a state exhibition of national pride and prestige and one I felt had to be experienced in the flesh. So, after I'd watched some of the ceremony on the TV, I decided around mid-morning to make my way to Independence Square. I had to catch two trotros and then walk quite a way to reach it. As I started walking from the bus station nearest my destination, I was surprised to see an increasing number of people were walking towards me. I was definitely walking against the tide rather than with the flow. And the nearer I got to Independence Square, the greater the swell of people. It looked and felt like crowds leaving a premiership football match - and I'd just missed the game!

There was still a hive of activity along the street leading to the square though, with people selling Ghanaian flags and badges, hooting horns and, of course, selling street food. I must have walked about half a mile to reach Independence Square itself. The marching in the square had definitely ended by the time I arrived, but I was able to get a better feel for the place and for the event by actually being there. Police coaches, tanks and stately cars were scattered around a massive dusty square which had been cordoned off by low metal barricades. Uniformed men and women were everywhere: all decked out in their procession regalia, in uniform, white gloves, with highly polished buttons and squeaky clean shoes. They looked pristine and immaculate. The square was obviously where all the ceremonial marching had taken place but now everyone, including military and civilians, was milling around in the arena together.

A huge monumental stone arch stood majestically adjacent to the square with the words 'Justice and Freedom' carved across the top of it with the date AD 1957. Two stone stars of Ghana were perched right on top of the monument. It towered above the crowds. Rising above Independence Square on the opposite side to the arch, there was another striking piece of architecture. It was dome-shaped with horizontal structures across it. This feature housed the seating from which all the dignitaries gave their speeches and watched the parades. It was enormous and was draped in bands of black, green, and yellow ribbon – the colours of the Ghanaian flag. There were also flags flying from its top. Around the square itself, there were massive tiered concrete seating areas for the crowds. I sat in one of these for a while to get a feel for the place and an elevated view of the square. There were still a number of families sitting around in no hurry to leave. It was impressive and I wished I'd got there earlier to witness more of the parades and of the spectacle.

The end of marching, parading and speeches in Independence Square did not mark an end to the Independence Day celebrations though. Being right next to the beach, many of the crowd simply slipped out from the square and onto the beach. Here they mingled, talked, chilled, ate, drank, rode horses and swam in the sea, many of them still fully clothed. I've never seen so many people crammed onto a beach.

Despite the poverty which many people in Ghana continue to experience and the struggles of daily living, Ghanaians seem to know instinctively how to party and enjoy themselves. The mood of the day was infectious and it felt great to be amongst such a vibrant, hospitable, proud and colourful people. It's hard to imagine what it must have felt like being ruled by a foreign power, a power that believed it had the right to govern and to plunder the natural resources, mainly gold, cocoa, timber and people that the country owned. Through the ages, Ghana had been dominated and governed by various foreign invaders all seeking to exploit the riches it had in abundance. Ghana's colonial past has clearly shaped its political and geographical present and influences how its people view themselves and the rest of the world today.

In this respect, there remains a marked contract between northern and southern Ghana reflecting the legacy of colonialism when the southern ports and the coastal region were developed to export resources. The current infrastructure is also testament to the country's colonial past when railways were built like major arteries running north to south to enable the export of goods from the interior. Today, Ghanaians flock to the south in search of better opportunities whilst northern Ghana remains less developed with a weak infrastructure. National Government is based in Accra and Ghana has adopted English as the national language.

Ghanaians are aware of their historical roots and are concerned about how they are viewed globally. Some give this as a reason why they don't like to be photographed as they fear being perceived as a backward nation within the wider world.

On reflection, I understand why Independence Day is marked as ceremoniously and formally as it is and long may it continue to be so. It's a public holiday where people rejoice in the fact that they are free from foreign domination and are now responsible for their own destiny.

The black ink incident

I'd bought two new linen smocks from M&S to wear in Ghana. One was a beautiful turquoise blue, the other bright orange. They were loose fitting and fell shirt-like over my hips. I thought linen would be a cool fabric in the heat but I soon realised that they were not really suitable as they had three-quarter length sleeves - I eventually didn't wear anything which had sleeves at all.

I decided to wear the orange one for work first shortly after I'd started. It wasn't until mid-morning that Awo drew attention to my back. I twisted around and tugged at the smock to check it out. I was mortified to see black marks scrawled across the lower back. Initially, I hadn't a clue how the black marks had got there - the top was brand new! I felt embarrassed to be wearing something in work with unsightly, dirty marks on it. I was still new and it didn't present a good impression. There wasn't much I could do there to get rid of the marks and, once made aware of them, my mind focused on how they'd got there.

The light gradually dawned.
The back of the seats on some trotros have gaps at the bottom and so anyone sitting behind could see and touch your lower back. My smock (as it wasn't tucked in) must have been visible and within easy reach of the person sitting behind me on my way into work. For whatever reason, someone had thought it a good idea to scrawl a black marker pen over my

orange top as I was sitting on the trotro.

Mystery solved. It was annoying and upsetting to think that someone had done it and also to think that others on the trotro had witnessed the prank without saying anything. No real harm done I suppose and I'd live to tell the tale, but it wasn't a great experience and made me feel that not all Ghanaians were happy to see obronis in their country. Or maybe it was simply a non-racist prank not worth giving a second thought.

I scrubbed the top until it was nearly threadbare but the ink was permanent and despite my efforts, the marks, though slightly fainter, remained. The memory of the incident faded better than the marks, but every time I subsequently travelled on a trotro, I checked the nature of the seat I was sitting on and was always conscious of who was sitting behind me. I probably gave them a knowing look too.

It never happened again.

Visit to the Katapor Schools, March 1st 2012

As I've mentioned, my placement at GNECC didn't directly involve visiting many schools in Ghana. Fortunately though, Awo arranged for me to accompany a group of officers from a number of different African countries – including Nigeria, Gambia, Zambia, Malawi and Ghana – who were visiting two Ghanaian schools as part of the Action Aid project they were involved in to promote children's rights. The schools were located in the Katapor community, Ga West Municipal District of Greater Accra.

In this context, there is a special set of rights for children and young people worldwide called the 'United Nations Convention on the Rights of the Child'. The United Nations (UN) approved this Convention on 20th November 1989 and it's now an international agreement that countries sign up to obey. Once countries agree to uphold the convention they are legally bound to what it says.

The UN Convention on the Rights of the Child has 54 articles and each article outlines a different right covering four main groupings: survival, protection, development and participation. Article 28 says that children have a right to education.

The aim of the visit to the Katapor schools was to enable those involved in the project to get a feel for what was actually going on in schools at the grass roots level and to test out some of the instruments (questions/research methods) which would be used in the project. In this respect, it was appreciated that to promote children's rights would mean talking to the children about them, as well as adults, and seeking their views and opinions.

After a long coach journey of over two hours on some pot holed, un-made and dusty roads, particularly in the latter stages, we eventually found the Katapor schools, located in spacious grounds with expansive views over the countryside. There were two schools which shared the same site: a primary school providing Basic Education for children aged 6-11 years and a Junior High School for pupils aged 12-14 years. My first impressions were that the buildings were all single-storey and looked dilapidated with well-worn paint and crumbling brickwork. On arrival, we received a warm welcome and brief talk by the head teacher. This was followed by a tour of the school. My initial thoughts as we walked around were of the poor general quality not only of the buildings, but also of the resources and facilities.

The library, where we all initially congregated, had so few books and was shabbily uninviting. What books there were had been jammed together in no apparent order on tatty wooden bookshelves. There were old PCs gathering dust, inaccessibly jumbled on top of the books on high shelves. Seating consisted of old wooden benches and long wooden tables.

The dilapidated nature of the classrooms was striking. They had precious few resources. Old, poor quality blackboards and chalk were used and the ceilings in a number of the classrooms had gaping holes in desperate need of repair. One classroom had paper chains strewn across the ceiling almost as if they were intended to cheer up the state of the ceiling. Some of the windows had wire mesh to keep out the mosquitoes whilst others simply had brown horizontal wooden slats, which offered no protection at all from mosquitoes but provided a little shade. As we walked past the windows in some classrooms, where the teacher had not arrived, inquisitive faces and big brown doe-eyes were peering out through the wooden slats to catch a glimpse of the visitors. Younger children sat at dilapidated wooden tables on small wooden chairs whilst older children sat in pairs at desks to which the seating was attached.

There were rotas on the walls outside classrooms listing the names of the pupils who would fetch water each day of that week. There were also signs in the school grounds reminding the children to *'Speak Good English'*.

The staffroom was small with again, few resources. Noticeboards were shabby and everything on them was handwritten, including the teaching timetable. Things simply looked worn out and in desperate need of updating or replacement.

What shocked me most was the appalling state of the toilets, which consisted of an area marked out by brick walls which both sexes were expected to use. There was no toilet as such, just a hole in the concrete at floor level behind brick walls. It was disgusting and offered no privacy or dignity for the children and especially for older girls.

In the kitchen area, huge cauldrons were used to make a starch-based meal for the children as part of the Government's feeding programme.

The school gave us coconut juice to refresh us - the coconuts were cut by one of the students using a machete type knife. I feared for his fingers but he was very adept.

Before we started our discussion groups, the students lined up in the open space outside the classrooms. All the children at the school wore uniform. Girls were neatly presented in brown gymslips with pale orange T shirts. They all wore short white socks. The boys wore long brown shorts and orange T shirts. They lined up in parallel rows of about ten to fifteen pupils, each precisely an arm's length behind one another, stretching an arm out to check they were the correct distance apart. I was impressed with how well behaved they all were.

Then the visitors divided into three groups. One group went off to discuss issues with parents, one with teachers and one, including me, with pupils.

What the children said

What follows is my personal summary of the issues the students collectively drew our attention to and what they said.

Initially, we had a class of about thirty boys and girls, aged between 12 and 14 years. Later in the day, they were split into gender groups. I chose to join a group of girls who elaborated on the themes which had come out earlier in the mixed group. I've integrated these comments so have more information about what the girls said overall. The education of girls is a major focus in Ghana because traditionally and culturally, their education has been considered less important than that of boys so I was happy to spend more time listening to what the girls had to say.

Students were prompted and asked questions mostly relating to the problems they faced getting to and in school and how they got support.

At first they were reluctant to talk and it was the boys who spoke out first. With encouragement, the girls offered their thoughts and after a short while, the whole group became more animated. In the all girls' group, some were more forward than others but they supported one another and elaborated on the themes that came out of the earlier session.

The role of parents

The ability of parents to support their children's education and schooling is an issue as parents don't have the money to support them. They often can't provide money for food, extra classes and text books. There are different pressures on, and expectations of, boys and girls. Students claimed that mothers expect girls to do more work in the home than boys and often kept their daughters at home to do a variety of chores. Girls' parents don't always look after them in the same way that they do boys and they have less parental support. They may be expected to fetch water or crack stones in the quarry which are used for construction work. They may have to work in a shop, take cassava to market, sell water or goods in the street and so many girls miss school. Girls are expected to do these chores even if they feel ill.

The work the girls are expected to do at home is often hard and tiring, so they have little energy for school work or study.

The challenge of getting to school

Many students live far from their school and have to walk there which also leaves them very tired when they arrive. On the way to school, clothes get dirty, smelly and sweaty which can lead to teasing from other pupils. This can be upsetting.

As if getting to school wasn't difficult enough, many of the children also highlighted the potential for snake bites and being attacked by men on their way there. Some girls are raped or beaten en route by boys and men. As a result, girls are afraid to go to school and don't want to go. To overcome their fear, they try to go in groups or simply run.

The rainy season makes getting to school even more difficult and often, once the children get themselves there, their books are dirty or damaged. As a result, some children opt to miss school entirely during the rains.

How students are treated in school

Pupils claimed that some teachers use the cane in school. Girls in particular emphasised this as the one thing they didn't like about their school. They thought there was too much caning.

They are punished if they don't have their

books, don't do well in tests, or if they don't have PE kit – to name only three.

Girls stressed they didn't like corporal punishment or being asked for money for canes, dusters, padlocks and lights. (Schools can expect financial contributions from parents for these items.) They wanted to know why teachers were punishing them.

Another punishment claimed to be administered by teachers would be to pinch them, make them kneel down or do weeding in the school grounds. (A better alternative to the cane, but it's important to remember that many of the weeds sting and cause itching.)

If the girls mis-behave they said they could be '*sacked*' (expelled) from the school.

Girls said that '*touching goes on*'. If it happens at home, they report it to their parents but there isn't a police station nearby to report such things.

Peer to peer issues

Pupils talked about friends and peers who would gossip if they were not dressed well or came to school dirty and smelly due to the long walk.

Girls might gossip about boys' hair and boys might criticise girls' bodies saying they are '*skinny, snake-like or their bottoms are too small*'. (Much giggling, some coyness and more shouting out as these issues were discussed!)

There is also laughter in the classroom if

someone can't answer a question.

Support for students in the home and at school

In school, girls said that they sometimes report teachers for the abuse they receive or for inappropriate behaviour but the teachers punish them and tell their parents. Parents didn't always help. Sometimes girls tell the elders in the community or family members but this would more often be an uncle rather than other girlfriends or their mother as they wouldn't take any notice. (*'They won't mind you'.*) The girls couldn't explain why they preferred to talk to their father's brother rather than their father. They didn't feel they could go straight to the Chief of the Community either.

They said that sometimes they would tell the headteacher about abuse in school.

What the girls liked about school

The girls were asked what they thought was positive about the school and said the teachers teach very well and that they dress properly. They enjoyed sports, the library, felt that discipline was good and valued worship; they also liked the end of term party.

My reflections on what the students revealed

It was frustrating to listen and to know there was little that would be done immediately to change the situation at the Katapor schools.

It's clear there are real and significant barriers to overcome before all children in Ghana are treated equally and all have their right to education met. It was also clear that young people's rights were being violated and that there were no effective systems in place to enable them to report abuse or to protect them.

From what was said, it wasn't difficult to appreciate why some children opted out of school and miss out on much of their education. It was hard to listen to their stories and reflect on the hardships they experience without feeling moved, without wishing the situation for children could be improved, and without wanting to support change for the better. The conditions for girls seemed particularly harsh and the punishments administered by the school for perceived misdemeanours, extreme and cruel but change of attitudes and cultural norms does take time.

The issue of abolishing corporal punishment in schools in Ghana is a challenging one. Ghana signed up to the UN Convention on the Rights of the Child and ratified it in February 1990. Whilst successive Governments say they uphold the abolition of corporal punishment in schools, it is still used in too many and there is clearly more work to be done to prevent the physical abuse of children.

GNECC has advocated against the use of corporal punishment together with Action Aid and other partners and has sought to promote, through training and the provision of information packs and resources, a Positive Discipline approach as an alternative and appropriate tool to manage pupil behaviour. This discipline model focuses on the positive aspects of behaviour, based on the belief that there are no bad children, just good and bad behaviours.

In terms of support systems, I felt the girls were very vulnerable and had no-one who they could turn to for support or could trust. I felt concerned that some teachers who were meant to support and enable all children and young people to thrive and develop were neither role models nor approachable and didn't protect the youngsters in their care.

On a positive note, through the work and awareness raising of NGOs, including GNECC, children and young people in Ghana are becoming more aware of their rights and slowly, the conditions in schools will, I feel, I hope, improve.

There are many, many issues which need to be resolved in Ghana to ensure that all children receive their entitlement to a quality basic education. Although I have described the situation and what the children think about two of the schools in the Katapor community, I know there are many that are far worse in Ghana and many children are still taught under trees. The two main issues which Ghana has grappled with over the years are access to basic education and the quality of education. Treating children with the dignity and humanity they deserve is equally important.

The country is and will continue, I'm sure, to make progress in these areas. In the meantime, I would suggest that we in the UK can all feel fortunate and grateful for the quality of the education system which our country provides.

Accra Mall

Address: Tetteh Quarshie and Spintex Road, East Airport, Accra

In the early days of my stay in Accra, I often visited Accra Mall. It's one of the largest and most modern indoor shopping malls in West Africa having been commissioned in 2008. It's located next to a complex road system called the Tetteh Quarshie interchange. (Named after a pre-independence Ghanaian agriculturist called Tetteh Quarshie.) The Mall majestically overlooks the interchange with its amazing motorway and road network and stands just off the Spintex Road. It's a busy area at all times of the day and night and particularly during morning and evening rush hours.

Tetteh Quarshie interchange (pronounced Tetta Kwarshee) used to be the Akuafo circle which was the largest roundabout in Ghana. The interchange is a vast architectural project built to cope with and ease the huge volume of traffic in the area. It's where the main Accra-Aburi road and the Accra-Tema motorway intersect. Various road networks now feed into Tetteh Quarshie interchange bringing traffic from all over Accra.

The major road project began in 2003, opened in February 2005 and was completed in May of that year. Technically speaking, Tetteh Quarshie is called a 'cloverleaf' interchange because of the loop pattern the major roads make which resembles a four leaved clover.

According to a news report on 27th February 2005 when the interchange opened to traffic, there was chaos. This was partly due to motorists' ignorance about using the junction and also due to lack of clear signage. I can well imagine the scene!

The report by MC Modern Ghana on the opening of the interchange read as follows:

> *'With the exception of the under-the-bridge Liberation Road, where vehicles from Legon to Accra moved freely without let-up or difficulty, traffic wardens from the Motor Traffic and Transport Unit (MTTU) of Ghana Police Service were all over the place to direct motorists to make the right detours on the six leg interchange from Accra, Legon, Achimota, Tema, Spintex Road and HIPC Junction. Obviously confused, motorists, who had run into wrong lanes shouted for help from policemen and pedestrians. Also, with only few of the stops completed, passengers in transit complained about long distances to walk before getting on other vehicles to their final destinations.'*

You may wonder why I'm waxing lyrical and long about a road system. The reason is that the whole area around Tetteh Quarshie, including the road network, is such a well-known landmark and is dear to my heart because I used to pass through it every day on my way to and from work.

On my way home from work, I'd often get off the trotro at the stop called 'Spanner' (short for Spanner Junction and the stop before Shangri-la) at Tetteh Quarshie roundabout. I have no idea why it was given this name, like many landmarks in Accra! From the Spanner trotro stop, I'd cross the infamous Liberation Road dual carriageway and walk up to Accra Mall to browse around before walking back to Roman Ridge where I lived. I could have taken a trotro back to Roman Ridge but often preferred to walk.

Despite being about a half hour walk from Accra Mall to the flat, I did it on many occasions after work and enjoyed it. Usually, the sun would be setting as I walked home passing what became familiar shops/stalls along the roadside en route. The fading light produced skies filled with a range of colour from powder blue through to pale purple, mauve, pink and orange where the sun was setting overlain by darker, sometimes almost navy blue clouds. Often the blue expanse of sky would look like the ripples you'd see in sand when the tide goes out. The beauty of the sky was a phenomenon I appreciated each and every time I walked home at dusk.

Being near the equator, the sun sets every day at around 6.00 pm all year round so I was often walking home in fading light watching the setting sun. Sometimes I'd stop at a spot on the way back and have a bottle of Star.

Alternatively, I might walk to Accra Mall

from the flat in Roman Ridge at some point over the weekend or catch a trotro. I'd get on the trotro I'd take to work and alight at the terminus. From there it would take about ten minutes to walk to the Mall. The route entailed crossing the notorious dual carriageway to Shangri-la, walking under a bridge which spanned the dual carriageway and then walking along Splinters road passed street sellers up to the Mall.

Back to Accra Mall itself. It stands proud in an elevated position adjacent to the Tetteh Quarshie interchange. It has a huge parking area on either side of the complex for over 900 cars to accommodate its many visitors and tourists. The Mall has two entrances and is close to Airport West where Mungo lived. (You'll be introduced to him later.)

Time Out says:
Posted: Fri Jul 19 2013

> '*Clothing boutiques, global sports brands and high-end furniture outlets populate the ground floor of Ghana's largest shopping mall. Glamorous African-inspired fashions fill the racks of Kiki Clothing and Jil Boutique, and a branch of African fabric specialists Woodin and Vlisco have a good range of prints. Also on the ground floor find familiar brands such as Levis, Puma and Swatch. A small food court includes fried chicken outlet Barcelo's and upmarket bar and restaurant Rhapsody's, and kids can let off steam in a central play area with a bouncy castle. Upstairs is the*

> *territory of Silverbird, which runs a well-stocked book and music store, Ghana's only multiplex cinema showing current blockbusters, Nollywood and Ghanaian films, and now a new bar Silver Lounge.'*

Compared to the Trafford Centre, White Rose or Meadow Hall, Accra Mall is tiny, but it's the biggest and best indoor shopping complex that Ghana has. There's also a branch of Eco Bank just outside the Mall which I used fairly regularly. The Mall extends over two levels and boasts two large supermarkets, one called 'Shopright' and the other 'Game Stores'. These were located at either end of the Mall on the ground floor. In-between these, there were a variety of shops selling wine, clothes, crocs, designer bags, jewellery, crafts, underwear, an Apple store, sportswear, cosmetics, swatch watches, household goods, Panasonic goods, a hairdresser/beauticians, pharmacy and more. I'm amazed I can recount nearly all the shops from one end of the Mall to the other but I can picture them all well and have a good memory! The prices of most things were exorbitant.

There was also an area on the ground floor which had a number of eating outlets including a good Thai restaurant and a children's play area. I discovered a special place in one of the fast food restaurants that sold ice cream in a great range of flavours, my favourites being coconut and vanilla. I treated myself quite regularly. On the first floor, there was a store which sold books, cards and CDs, and also a cinema complex. I never went to the cinema whilst I was in Accra.

Lining Splinters Road which led up to and passed Accra Mall, there was a range of street sellers and a taxi area. There was also a small trotro station set back from the main road. The various stalls would be selling second hand shoes, bags, mobile phones to name but a few and, of course, food at all hours of the day and night.

So what attracted me to the Mall and made me visit so often? Well it was fully air conditioned which was a bonus in the heat and had some nice toilets; it was beautifully clean and modern. I enjoyed window shopping and particularly liked to look in the book and CD store upstairs. I did quite a bit of food shopping in the supermarkets there too. I also needed to visit the Airtel guys who had a stand in the Mall to top up the air time and data on my mobile phone and memory stick. (I could only top up air-time and not data from the local shops in Roman Ridge.) I needed the latter to enable me to access the internet.

In addition, I particularly loved to look at all the beautiful Ghanaian fabric in the two up-market stores in the Mall which sold Ghana's most famous brands. These are Woodin and Vlisco. The Vlisco shop window displayed models wearing stunning designer dresses. The bold prints and modern designs didn't always look practical to wear with their flowing trains, elaborate shoulder motifs, billowing sleeves and/or elaborate pleats and folds but never failed to have the 'wow' factor. There was a wonderful variety of prints and patterns in bright, bold colours. The material felt strong and good quality. I bought fabric from the Woodin store in Accra Mall and had a number of outfits made for me. I designed my own flared skirt which I had made in a plain dark blue Woodin material and matched it with a simple sleeveless top made in a bold geometric pattern in blue and mauve to match the skirt. I also bought material which I had made into a traditional Ghanaian outfit consisting of the long skirt and matching top.

Happy days looking at and choosing Ghanaian fabric.

I also visited the hairdresser/beautician in Accra Mall twice and had a memorable experience on the second occasion which provided another story!

Living in Roman Ridge: Marching and the bats

Roman Ridge is a planned neighbourhood located in the north of Accra. It's considered to be one of the 'premier' locations to live in Ghana. As a consequence, the area is home to the affluent in Ghanaian society, top government officials, academics, big business owners, foreign incomers and ex-pats. Most of the residences are houses and apartments. There are also many embassies and administrations, major banks, hotels and famous restaurants in the area. The vicinity of Roman Ridge has a good road network with the majority of roads being well-tarred and landscaped with streetlights, walkways and tree-lined avenues. These streets have few potholes which make for a smooth ride around the area. (You do notice these things when you ride on trotros a lot!) For families there are schools in the area which cater for children from nursery to senior high school.

All the houses and buildings in Roman Ridge are connected to both the nation's public water and electricity mains and utility services in the area are claimed to be one of the best in the country.

I lived in a three-bedroomed flat on the second floor of a large block of flats in Roman Ridge. The flat had been donated by the Government of Ghana for use by VSO, so Ghanaians occupying the other flats in the block were civil servants working in various departments for the Ministry. The block had a central stairwell and four floors with flats either side of the stairwell. There were about five parallel blocks in total. Each block was positioned at right angles to a main road. The blocks were separated and surrounded by trees, low bushes and space in front of the blocks which was used for parking. My block was painted white but looked in dire need of a fresh coat of paint. This would have made a vast difference to its appearance and was blatantly obvious because an adjacent block had been repainted and looked so much more 'up market'.

I was fortunate indeed to be living in this 'plush' part of Accra, although not everyone living in Roman Ridge was well off.

Behind the block of flats where I lived, there was a low rise terrace consisting of workshops/garages and very simple homes with tiny windows which were occupied by the community, many of whom worked in the local shops in Roman Ridge. It was a small close-knit community who shared basic facilities. It was several months before I realised that they were actually homes as people accessed them from the side not facing the block of flats so I couldn't see anyone coming and going although the workshops/garages opened up towards the flats.

The small local shops which looked temporary and makeshift were about 500 yards away from the flats along the roadside opposite Roman Ridge Shopping Arcade and right next to a building site. The shops sold a range of household goods, basic foodstuffs and water. There was also a tiny spot and place where you could buy kebabs tucked away at the end of the row of shops and right next to the building site. I generally bought large bottles of water from the local shops, eggs, bread, small packets of biscuits for the local children, airtel time for my phone and mosquito spray. Being such a regular customer I got to know the people who served in the shops well.

(The arcade accommodated an odd mix of up-market expensive shops including those selling: shoes, home interiors, house plants, underwear, general gifts and a travel agent on one level with a couple of good restaurants and a pharmacy on the lower level.)

The local Ghanaians who lived behind the block of flats had very little space and appeared to have few material possessions. Most of the children I knew lived in these poorer dwellings and played in the open space outside the flats.

Often, early in the morning there would be women washing clothes and hanging them out to dry in the area in front of the workshops and our block of flats. Betty, who was a seamstress and made a number of outfits for me, lived in this local community and worked in one of the workshops. The small community was not typical of the residents of Roman Ridge as a whole.

Going back to where I lived in Roman Ridge, one of the best features of my accommodation was the balcony which, being on the second floor, afforded not only a lovely area to sit and soak up the fresh air, but also excellent views in the distance over Accra. I watched some amazing sunsets from that balcony and often enjoyed eating breakfast and dinner there or simply drinking a bottle of Star after a jog in the late afternoon. You could also see the Harmattan season approaching towards the end of November until mid-March (winter).

The Harmattan is the dry and dusty trade wind which blows down from the Sahara in the north to the Gulf of Guinea coast bringing with it a fine red dust. Looking into the distance from the balcony, the dust created a hazy fog which masked the detail and the outline of buildings and features previously clearly visible on the horizon. It was like a veil creeping imperceptibly towards Accra, carrying the dust which draped a silky red blanket over everything. The effect caused by the dust and sand stirred by these winds is known as the Harmattan haze.

At all times of year, dust was a constant in the flat. Even if you swept the tiled floor daily, there would be more the next day. But during the Harmattan, the dust was even thicker. The air also felt drier at this time and it was not apparently unusual to feel dryness in the throat. I didn't feel I suffered personally from the effects of the Harmattan or if I did, I wasn't aware. Maybe I swept my room a little more often. I did notice the change in the clarity of the view from our balcony though. The haze made the distant scene over Accra look mysterious, as if it was shrouded in a light muslin veil.

Another bonus of living in the flat in Roman Ridge was the fact that it was conveniently located - about a five minute walk - close to a spot which served food as well as drinks. It was called the

'Bouncey Eye's'. I went there quite regularly as the staff were friendly and they did a mean jollof rice with chicken. We were also fortunate to live within a ten minute walk of a Deli France. It catered for the more European taste in food and was one of the few places in Accra where you could buy a good cup of coffee or tea. It sold delicious bread, cakes and filled baguettes. It was a special treat to visit the Deli.

For me though, there were two particularly unique and noteworthy features to the location of my accommodation in Roman Ridge. One was its proximity to what would probably be the equivalent of a borstal or a reform centre for young people in the UK (although with a much stricter regime), the other, that it was directly beneath the flight path of a cloud of bats.

The borstal was one of several stopping off points for the trotros which passed through Roman Ridge en route to Nima (one of the inner city poor, unplanned areas) and central Accra. The pronunciation of the word borstal had to be correct though to gain recognition by the mates (the young men, who invariably wore the lowest slung jeans imaginable, taking fares on the trotro). They'd usually be holding a wad of notes and would yell out the next stop and final destination. So when on a trotro, you had to ask for 'Bor staaarr' to be understood – that was how it was pronounced. The borstal did appear to be somewhat of a boot camp and one where marching was definitely considered to instil both discipline and routine. In this respect, young inmates would have to get up between 3.00am and 4.00am to march around a square which was part of the borstal compound. Whilst this may have been considered an effective strategy to discipline the young boys and girls in the borstal, it also proved a disturbance and 'punishment' to innocent local residents who could be woken in the early hours by the shrill, staccato marching commands which pierced the clear still air. Whether or not marching was a favourite occupation of the inmates, it was, I'm sure, an unwelcome disturbance to the sleep patterns of local residents, including me. Although I have to confess that it probably bothered me more than the locals because Ghanaians tend to rise very early anyway.

There were other forms of noise pollution in Roman Ridge, quite aside from, but in addition to, the marching! One was created by the local building development. Whilst I was living in the flat there was an interesting capital development project taking place right on our doorstep – about 500 yards from where I lived. A huge new block of luxury flats was being built to create a high rise development along the main road leading up to the small group of local shops opposite Roman Ridge shopping arcade.

The posters outside the building development advertising the apartments and facilities showed the palatial interiors of the proposed new homes with modern furniture and beautiful, high specification fixtures and fittings. There were also plans for a fitness centre, underground parking and a rooftop leisure facility. It all looked extremely desirable and the views from the apartments at the top of the building over the city would be phenomenal.

These luxury apartments would provide a stark contrast to the dwellings of the adjacent small community.

In the process of construction, periodically, deliveries and work would take place all through the night. At such times, machines would be droning and floodlights would be on, men would be shouting, concrete mixers grinding away and engines whirring, creating plenty of noise and disturbance. When this happened it was as bad as the marching, if not worse, and made it very hard to get any sleep.

I did discuss this with a Ghanaian neighbour on one occasion, but learned there was no effective building control service, or its equivalent, and so nobody could do a thing about it.

Another, but very different noise irritant was created by the local canine community. Occasionally, and probably when local bitches were on heat, there would be a chorus of dogs barking within ear-shot of the flat. It would begin in the middle of the night. What was so annoying was that the barking would start, then abate for a while, only to start again just as you were falling asleep. The barking was always intermittent and one dog would appear to set off the rest. No-one seemed to be bothered as this would go on for what seemed like an age with nothing being done to quieten the animals.

One time I did get out of bed to try to see if I could do anything. I walked down from the second floor of the flat to go out in the dark to see which dogs were making the noise and to try to disperse them. I discovered the culprits and threw some stones in their general direction to move them on which worked. Based on this positive outcome, my subsequent strategy was to collect a few stones from outside and keep these on the coffee table on the balcony for such times when the barking occurred during the night. Random hurling of small stones in the general direction of the barking did, usually, work wonders, and for that, much thanks!

As for the bats, these were an incredible spectacle which had to be seen to be believed. In terms of the visible display, I would liken them to the famous Brighton starlings. Come dusk around 6.00pm each evening in March when I arrived at Roman Ridge, the sky would gradually fill with tiny black flapping specks. They came from an area known as 37 which was about a 25 minute walk away. It was an area which had a trotro station, a hospital, a few shops, an open market and a Max Mart supermarket.

At first there would be the odd one or two in the sky as sparse specks, and then they grew and grew in density until they looked like a swathe of black fluttering specks filling the sky. They created a cloud of frenetically flapping and squealing small black specks, coming together, swirling around in one direction and then another only to part and re-group in a never ending swarm in the sky.

During the course of the year, the flight path of the bats must have changed as they all disappeared during the summer months. Myth apparently has it that the bats used to live further north where an Ashanti Chief lived. When the Ashanti Chief died and was brought to Accra to be buried, it is believed that the bats followed him.

(Chieftaincy is officially accepted in Ghana and relates to the historic structures in place to govern regions in Ghana. Ashanti is one sub-group of the Akan tribe. Politicians ask Chiefs for advice and liaise with them as they're usually closer to the people and extremely well respected within their communities.)

Other interesting features of the flat in Roman Ridge

Compared to the hideous experiences I had in Kenya with accommodation, the flat where I lived in Ghana was a palace. In this respect, it was spacious, light and didn't leak when it rained!

It was also well furnished with a large dining table, leopard print sofa and matching chairs, plus a spare double bed mattress (all incredibly dusty but comfortable) in the shared living space and a desk, chair, double bed and wardrobe in each of the three bedrooms.

There was also a shared bathroom/toilet.
The kitchen was quite small and it didn't have a cooker that worked, but the hob did and we also had a fridge and an array of basic pots, pans, plates and cutlery.

Cockroaches were not unknown in Accra although, thankfully, not too common in the flat. You'd find the odd one lurking in the kitchen behind a pot or a jar and the occasional specimen in the bedroom but, overall, they were not too prevalent. The biggest insect scourge, next to the dreaded mosquito, was ants.

Ants were quite simply ubiquitous. If you left a crumb out in the kitchen, it would be the site of an army of ants within minutes. The bags we used for rubbish would be full of them. Whole armies of ants would also march, in military fashion, across various stretches of the walls in the flat. They seemed to have a particular penchant for electrical points which I found quite intriguing. I once watched a long horizontal trail near the ceiling which stretched from one wall in my bedroom all the way to another; they were rampant. Samina, my flatmate, was also invaded in her bed a couple of times. It made my skin crawl when she told me but I was fortunate they never ventured into my bed.

It was something I remember making a mental note of when I returned home. I was in my mother's kitchen, making a cheese sandwich and realised, when I'd made it, that I didn't have to immediately put the bread away, that food left out in the kitchen wouldn't become the target for an ant invasion. I remember smiling to myself with relief at the realisation.

Ants and cockroaches aside, there were, of course, mosquitoes – despite the fine mesh netting which was put up at every window. I was lucky that my bedroom had its own toilet and shower (it would be a bit too grand to call it an en suite) which was located off a small space next to my bedroom where I could hang clothes to dry. The outer wall to this area was made of breeze blocks with open spaces within them. This, of course, meant that this area was exposed to the outside and provided an open invitation to mosquitoes. Despite there being a door to the toilet and shower, the breeze blocks provided a poor barrier and as a consequence, it was usual for me to shower with at least two mosquitoes.

I distinctly remember one occasion when I went to the loo early in the morning and must have been half asleep leaving both my legs exposed only to find them covered with bites later in the day. I had about six on each leg. In more 'with it' moments on the loo, I would be on guard and would flap a towel or something around my legs to ward off the lethal little pests. Not surprisingly, I went through quite a few cans of mosquito spray during my stay.

Damp was also a strangely deceptive feature of the flat. I discovered this to my dismay when I returned to Ghana following a trip back to the UK in August 2012. I'd left my laptop in the flat, lovingly wrapped in a soft winceyette type of material and placed in a drawer in my wardrobe. On my return, half the keys on my laptop wouldn't work and I needed a new keyboard to solve the problem. This problem, I was informed by the IT guy who eventually (months later) fixed it, was caused by damp. Further evidence of damp was the fact that a thin green film of mould would grow on anything made of leather which was left unused for any length of time.

I did manage to do one thing to improve the flat before I returned home. Not long before I left, after some gentle persuasion from me, the whole flat received a fresh coat of paint (pale yellow throughout) courtesy of VSO and particularly Anita who worked for VSO and was responsible for all things related to administration, house maintenance and safety. Regardless of the drips of paint all over the floors which we needed to sort ourselves and getting rid of all the empty tins of paint the workmen had left behind on the balcony, it made the flat look a whole lot brighter and fresher.

    Despite all the creatures who shared the flat, the cold water in the shower, and issues which Val (flatmate when Samina left) and I latterly had actually getting water in the flat, I have fond memories of living there and of those I shared the flat in Roman Ridge with.

VSO flatmates

The turnover of volunteers in the flat was constant as new ones arrived and those who'd finished their placements left.

When I initially moved into Roman Ridge, Samina was my sole flatmate. Although from Oxford in the UK and British, her father was Indian and her mother from Finland (I think). This gave her an interesting cultural background. She had beautiful olive skin and short jet black hair. She'd been living in the flat for nearly a year so knew all the ropes. She was gregarious, feisty, laughed a lot and was a good cook. She also had an extensive collection of handmade dresses made from an array of vibrant Ghanaian material. She introduced me to Betty, our local dressmaker. Samina loved to dance and was interested in various alternative therapies. She did some reiki on my shoulder which helped and which I appreciated. In the early days, before Rhys moved in, we exercised together in the spare bedroom, to a video on her laptop. She was 'expert' at downloading films and would regularly share one with me. She adopted and adored a little dog she called Madge who lived outside the flat.

After a few weeks, Rhys moved into the third bedroom for part of the week. His placement with Christian Aid required him to split his time between Accra and Koforidua (Kof for short) and whilst in Accra, he was based in Roman Ridge with Samina and me. Rhys was tall, slim and had a goatee beard and moustache. His manner was calm and measured and he had a dry (Yorkshire) sense of humour. His family hailed from Sheffield and he supported the city's football team although 'back home' he lived in London. He was also a good conciliator. He was easy going and easy to get along with. In fact you often weren't aware that he was in the flat, maybe due to his more transient status.

His partner, Lizzie, who was also a volunteer, was based in Kof. She too stayed at Roman Ridge quite often when Rhys was there as Accra offered more opportunities for sightseeing and going out at the weekend. Lizzie had long, light brown hair, more often than not tied back in a high ponytail. She usually wore dark-framed glasses which made her look studious and less fun than she actually was. She was a warm person who was a pleasure to know and to talk to. (Her mum was also called Barbara so we seemed to have a connection through that fact.) Lizzie was keen to keep fit, was energetic and a good listener. She took up jogging in the early mornings when she was staying in the flat.

Rhys, Lizzie and me would often go to a spot and drink Star together, chill, talk and watch the world go by. I was drinking with them in a spot in Airport West on Sunday, 8th July 2012 whilst watching Andy Murray lose to Roger Federer in the final at Wimbledon. It was such a huge disappointment and an afternoon none of us will forget, despite drinking quite a few bottles of Star between us!

Being near the airport, (about a 25 minute walk away) our Roman Ridge flat proved a busy staging post for volunteers flying into Ghana en route north and for those flying out of the country. Many would stay the night, sleeping in a spare bedroom if one was available or on the spare double mattress which lived stacked up against a wall in the living room.

So for several months, Samina, Rhys and me shared the flat in Roman Ridge, together with Lizzie some weekends and various volunteers who'd stay over-night and then move on.

Towards the end of my time in Ghana, Samina left, Lizzie moved in with Rhys on a more or less permanent basis, as her work allowed, and Val moved into Samina's former room.

Val was from the Philippines and was undertaking research on the impact of VSO's work. He was a quiet and amiable person who cooked rice a lot. He often left a pan of rice on the hob with a lid on it, but despite the lid, when you looked inside, the white rice would be alive with little black writhing specks….yep, ants! This didn't seem to deter him from cooking more rice though. I remember he cooked us all a meal of sticky chicken wings the first Sunday he was in the flat. They were delicious. He told me his grandmother had taught him how to cook and to my way of thinking, she'd done a really good job.

Val spent much of his time in his own room on his laptop as well as watching football on the TV. He liked to party though and knew the community of Filipinos who were based in Accra. The volunteers from the Philippines tended to bond and gravitate to one another. They'd go out as a group or meet up most weekends.

Sharing accommodation wasn't always easy but it was one of the conditions of acceptance of a VSO placement - that you'd be required to share. It had its ups and downs, but at the end of the day, it was great to meet and live with such an intelligent, caring, motivated, diverse and interesting group of people.

Madge, Spot, Brownie and Fatty

It was an odd mix of pleasure and irritation to be pestered by the stray dogs that lived outside the block of flats. It was deceptively easy to become attached to the attention they freely gave, even if at times it was unwanted. In the beginning, there were four small, whippet-like dogs who roamed around the area outside our block. We christened them Madge, Spot, Fatty, and Brownie. They were the best of friends and each had a distinctive character.

Fatty, as his name suggests, looked the best fed and was brown and white. He was the youngest, most playful and could be a handful when he jumped up, smearing the red dust from his paws over your legs and clothes in the process. His rounded belly would waddle from side to side as he got excited and started jigging around when he saw you. Maybe he had worms; it was quite probable.

Spot was named, tongue in cheek, because he had none and was brown all over. He had an obsession with vehicles and, from the outset, had an obvious death wish. No matter how hard we tried to encourage him otherwise, he would stalk passing cars and motorcycles. He'd crouch, head resting on his front paws, eyes fixated on his prey until the vehicle approached and then would chase full pelt after it until it outpaced him. His antics were horrendous to watch and you knew that one day... In quieter, non-vehicle stalking moments, Spot loved to be stroked behind his ears. He'd appear to go off into a trancelike state. It was entertaining to watch as his eyelids slowly drooped and he soaked up the attention. He was Rhys' favourite dog.

Brownie, who was also plain brown in colour, had clearly been abused at some stage as he wouldn't allow anyone to get near or touch him. He was timid and painfully thin with a protruding ribcage. I think he'd probably been hit by a car in the past as he limped quite badly on one of his back legs.

Of the four dogs, Madge was special and Samina doted on her. She was black and white, skinny, fragile, bright as a button and craved attention. She had appealing eyes, bat like ears, a beautiful little face and would do anything to please. She too had been injured, probably in a road accident as her back-end was incredibly emaciated and she hopped around barely using one of her hind legs.

All the dogs looked mangy and flea-bitten - and they probably were - as they roamed wild and didn't appear to have owners. They were just free roaming spirits. I would never stroke or hug them for fear of catching anything but I'd always speak to them and give them a gentle pat on the head or stroke behind the ears.

I suppose the dogs loved obronis because we are on the whole, by nature, animal and dog lovers whereas Ghanaians are, on the whole, not. I don't think the Ghanaians could quite fathom the attention we gave to the dogs or how much we seemed to like them. This feeling was completely mutual as the dogs would bound up to see us whenever we arrived home and make such a fuss. They never greeted Ghanaians in this way. In fact they reacted in quite the opposite manner and would shy away from the locals.

It's interesting to reflect on the different treatment and attitude to animals, in particular dogs, Ghanaians have compared to Brits. As a nation we adore our pets and get particularly upset about animal mistreatment. We have charity shops for dogs as well as charities to support donkeys and cats and are aware of endangered animal species around the world. I was recently amazed myself at our level of pandering to animals when I walked into a brand new large store which sold goods solely for the dietary, play, and clothing needs of dogs and other animals. It had jars of chews and treats for dogs which were displayed exactly like the jars of sweets you might buy for children. The store was called, maybe not surprisingly, 'Barkers'!

But in a country where poverty and low standards of living are major issues, it's not so hard to understand why dogs and animals are not viewed as a high priority for love, affection and attention. They are incidental to the lives of the vast majority of the people there. From my own experience, dogs are either kept as guard animals in the palatial residences that exist in some areas of Accra like Airport West, or are left to fend for themselves where they roam – just like Madge, Spot, Fatty and Brownie.

And, back to our dogs. Madge and Spot were definitely a couple and would nearly always be seen together. The four dogs would gamble around, chase one another and seemed to have a great time despite their obvious poverty, probable hunger and apparent homelessness. They were entertaining to watch although their attention seeking did, as I said, sometimes get on your nerves and you would often end up shooing them away as they got under your feet. Of course they weren't trained and that fact was brought home clearly to me one day when I threw a stick for one of them to fetch. I was given a look which said, '*What on earth did you do that for and what do you expect me to do…run after a stick?*' It made me smile. How naive was I?

After a little while, Madge and Spot took to following us if we walked anywhere locally. They even followed Samina and me one evening when we walked to a concert at a local venue called Alliance Francaise. Because the roads had few pavements we would try to encourage the dogs to go back but they ignored us and simply followed at their leisure. When we arrived at the Alliance Francaise, the pair stood outside the gates with pained expressions on their faces as if to say, '*Why can't we join you, is this the end of the road?*' They were soon shooed away by the Ghanaians who stood on guard at the gates on reception. We'd been walking for a good twenty minutes to get to the Alliance Francaise and hoped the dogs would be able to find their own way back. Thankfully, the next day we discovered they had.

As the dogs got to know us, they became more daring and even took to coming into the entrance to the block of flats and climbing the internal stairway. To our amusement, they took to sunbathing on a small balcony area on the first floor just off the stairwell which was not accessible to humans. The dogs would have to squeeze through the open spaces in the breezeblocks to reach it. From there they would stretch out to sunbathe, peer down on the community and from their elevated position, watch the world go by.

Sadly, one by one, the dogs disappeared. Fatty was the first. One day he was there, then, quite suddenly, he wasn't. He just wasn't around anymore. Soon after that Brownie went walkabout. Next was Spot. We liked to think that they'd just decided to move on to pastures new but deep down we knew otherwise.

So in time, Madge was the only little dog of the infamous four left, although there were other strays that appeared on the scene from time to time. On one occasion, when Madge was on heat, I saw her quite literally 'hooked up' with one of the strays. I felt sorry for her and, not surprisingly, she became 'with puppy'. She struck a lonely figure now and was even more demanding of attention, bounding up to me when I arrived home from work with even greater excitement and she was always there to greet me in the morning.

People on the second floor flat opposite us started to leave left over take-away food for her outside their door and we would feed her too as her tummy swelled ever so slightly in her fragile little frame. I was looking forward to seeing her puppy, a baby Madge. As the pregnancy progressed she became more cautious in her manner and wouldn't follow me far from the community on her own.

One sad Friday evening, poor Madge died. She was knocked down on the road outside the block of flats. I was with her when it happened and saw her just after she'd been hit. I'd decided to walk to the Alliance Francaise to go to a poetry and dance evening. I'd just given Madge a doggy chew after leaving (I'd bought a packet for her) and she began to follow me. Then, as I said, being more cautious on her own, she stopped to go back towards the flats as I carried on walking. It was dark, but something made me look back and I saw what I thought was her in the distance lying in the road. At first I wasn't sure it was Madge and certainly didn't want to believe it was. I felt a sudden sense of panic and rushed back only to find it was her. There was no blood and her eyes were open but she was lifeless. I think a people carrier had hit her and had driven off without stopping. The driver probably didn't see her or didn't care. It was only a dog after all. I couldn't bring myself to touch her and didn't know what to do. I felt utterly powerless. I phoned Val and he came out but there was nothing either of us could do. Before Val arrived on the scene, Madge struggled to lift her tiny head off the ground a little as if she was trying to get up for me, but then she slumped back down and was completely still.

Then, a strange local man who I believe had a mental illness and who used to hover around the community all day appeared on the scene and prodded Madge's motionless little body. I wanted to shout at him to stop, but I don't think he realised that she'd gone. He seemed to think he could bring her back to life by prodding her but of course he couldn't. There was nothing anybody could do. Eventually, he picked her up quite callously by her four skinny legs, her head flopped back and swayed from side to side. He took her to an area behind the flats and buried her there whilst Val and I looked on. I felt an incredible and quite disproportionate sense of loss when Madge died and was overwhelmed by the fragility and unpredictability of life. One minute Madge was skipping up to see me and I was feeding her a chew and the next minute she was dead.

  I realised how attached I was to her. For several weeks it was painful to leave the apartment with no Madge to greet me in the mornings and equally sad to return with no Madge to rush up and fuss around me in the evening. Such is our temporary existence on earth. The loss of Madge was even more heartfelt as I'd been looking forward to her giving birth. I never did get to see that little baby Madge. For weeks after her death, the strange man who buried her would cross himself whenever he saw me and mumble words in Twi which I didn't understand.

Mungo: How the other half live

Unlike Madge and co. Mungo experienced how the other half lived in Ghana. I got to know him when a fellow volunteer, Jackie, introduced me to house and dog-sitting for ex-pats. Mungo lived in an ex-pat home that I looked after when his owners went away.

He was an Alsatian/retriever cross with the most beautiful thick, black shiny coat. The shine on his coat was attributable to his regular helpings of sardines which were mixed, on most days, with his dog biscuits. There were no scaly bald patches on him although ticks don't appear to differentiate between the haves and have-nots in this world, in Ghana at least, and Mungo was known to host a few now and again. Mungo was nearly a year old and full of life and energy when I met him and the prime motivating force in his life was to play. That included playing chase me with my ball, chase me without my ball, stroke me, tickle me, and play tug of war with any manky piece of rope or rag to hand. Or, if you like, let me take you for a walk where I can sniff out other dogs and strange smells to my heart's content along our route.

He lived in a large four bedroomed property in an upmarket area of Accra called Airport West with a spacious garden surrounding it. The house had hot running water, a generator, open plan living/dining room, kitchen with separate utility room, four large bedrooms, four bathrooms and the 'piece de resistance' - a swimming pool. It really was a great pad for a young dog to call home. There was also a huge playroom in the house which was full of books and every toy, craft, and educational game imaginable.

To assist with the management and security of Mungo's home there was a guard on the high-gated entrance; a cook/nanny; a cleaner who lived in separate premises within the grounds, and a gardener. Mungo's main playmates were the two children who also lived in the house with him, their parents and Max, his friend, an older black Labrador who visited regularly and who Mungo visited in return.

Unlike Madge and co, who were complete free spirits and determined their own daily agendas, Mungo had routines. He was fed daily in the morning and evening and then walked, either by the gardener or by his owners. He was also taken, on mutually agreed days, to play at Max's home and reciprocal arrangements ensured Max also visited Mungo to keep him company whilst his owners were at work and the children at school. Each dog would be taken to the other's home in a chauffeur driven 4x4, which did, I have to say, seem somewhat of a luxury.

In terms of doggy games, Mungo, being the younger and more immature dog, was still coming to terms with his own sexuality and had clearly a lot to learn. He was also blissfully unaware of the laws against homosexuality in Ghana as one of his more passionate pursuits included trying to mate with Max on a regular basis. Max was having none of it, of course, and got quite exhausted trying to fend off Mungo's amorous and misplaced attention, especially outside in the heat of the Ghanaian sun. The two of them would romp around with Mungo chasing poor Max, they'd both stop, breathless for a water break, only for Mungo to resume his sexual harassment over and over again when he regained his energy.

My relationship with Mungo blossomed during the time I spent with him. It made me smile to be greeted by him each morning as I walked into the living room where he'd spent the night. He'd wag his tail to let me know he was pleased to see me and almost asked: did I want to play chase the ball? He loved to be chased around the furniture in the living room, usually with a ball or toy in his mouth taunting, 'come and catch me'. Also, from being a fairly untrained dog, I did encourage him not to jump up when he greeted me, or anyone else for that matter, a trait which would definitely put off a non-dog lover. He was way too big and powerful a dog for those puppy antics. I taught him some basic tricks like giving paws for treats (he was very bright) and I even managed to get him to walk to heel and without tugging too much. I didn't, however, manage to curtail his aggression towards other dogs. I wasn't quite sure how that was going to be addressed but was concerned when his high levels of testosterone and resultant aggression resulted, on one memorable occasion, in me using all my muscle to avoid being dragged under the wheels of a passing car. It happened when Mungo spotted a dog on the other side of the road when I was taking him for a walk and he lunged to attack. It was a scary experience and not one I was keen to repeat. He was an incredibly powerful dog who wasn't willing to give up on the chase without a battle with me. It took all my powers to control him as he lurched full pelt to get at the dog he saw as his adversary. A choker chain might have helped. Failing that, I think a visit to the vet for treatment to curtail, in one way or another, his high level of testosterone might have been a wise option to consider.

All things considered, Mungo's well-being was certainly well catered for and planned. It maybe seemed over the top in the context of there being so many children and adults living in Ghana who were struggling to survive. I did feel it was incongruous and over-indulgent but then again, having the resources to treat their dog in a pampered way was clearly the right of Mungo's owners, and he was a lovely dog. I just hope he appreciated how privileged he was. So, just as there are the haves and the have-nots in the human world in Ghana, it is also the case for the canine population.

It was, indeed, interesting to see how the other half lived.

Pink chickens

I couldn't believe my eyes as I returned home from work one day to find a puce pink hen strutting around pecking nonchalantly at the ground followed by a brood of about six puce pink chicks.

I hurriedly scrabbled in my bag to find my camera, feeling that I had to take photos to verify this amazing phenomenon. I literally shouted at them to stay put, but of course they carried on strutting calmly away from me in the direction they thought food might be, completely oblivious of my astonishment.

Camera in hand I stalked the mother hen and her chicks. I had to take photos. Who'd believe it? Pink chicks. They were such an amazing deep, puce pink colour and looked so pretty. Was this a new breed of chicken? I'd never seen anything like it.

Dashing up the stairs and into the flat feeling I'd made a remarkable discovery, I said to Val, 'Have you seen the colour of that hen and her chicks? They're puce.'

I was reliably informed that it was dye which had been used to mark the chicks so farmers would know who they belonged to. I felt incredibly naïve and just a little embarrassed but was able to laugh at myself for my ignorance. I think, at heart, I wanted them to be a new breed of beautiful, brightly coloured chicks. Trust the Ghanaians to use such a vibrant colour to mark their flock. They were certainly highly visible and added even more colour to our outdoor environment!

The eyebrow incident

What possessed me to do it that afternoon I'll never know.

I'm just not very good at plucking and shaping my eyebrows. I simply don't seem to be able to see the hairs very well. Anyway, I occasionally go to a beautician back in the UK to have my eyebrows done. I go to see Jude who knows I want nothing extreme, just to 'remove the stragglers' whilst keeping the natural shape. Once, she recommended that I have my eyebrows dyed a little darker to give them more definition. It was a recommendation I took and I was pleased with the results. It worked well as she was very cautious in putting a little colour on them, removing the colour to check the darkness, then adding a tad more colour as necessary: this is the context to my tale.

So, while I was in Ghana, I thought as a treat, I'd have my eyebrows done in the hairdresser-cum beauty salon in Accra Mall. I'd had my eyebrows tidied up there once before by a beautician who, well to be honest, looked like you'd generally imagine a beautician to look. You know, full make up, pretty, nice skin, etc. However, I was told that she wasn't working that day and the woman who was available was not someone you'd immediately think was a beautician. She was grossly over-weight, quite masculine in build and look. However, feeling I shouldn't be prejudiced, I decided to go ahead.

She asked me how I wanted my eyebrows done, with the alternatives on offer being a razorblade or waxing. I declined both and said plucking the few stragglers with a pair of tweezers would suit me fine. To this day I've no idea what she would have done had I selected the razor blade option. The mind boggles and surely, in hindsight, that was my cue to make a speedy exit.

She proceeded to pluck away with a pair of tweezers and I was okay with the end result, having stressed the removal of very few hairs and the requirement to look 'natural'. Then I must have had a moment of sheer madness. I asked if she could colour my eyebrows to make them more defined. Answering in the affirmative, she proceeded to dye them.

I'm sure back home, Jude only used a semi-permanent colour and I'm equally sure the 'beautician' in Accra Mall used a permanent black hair dye. She began the process by defining the shape she wished to colour by applying Vaseline around my eyebrows. Then the dye went on. I started to get a bit anxious after ten minutes or so but she checked how the colour was doing and suggested it needed a little longer. How trusting was I?

After about 15 minutes she removed the dye and suggested I look in the mirror to appreciate her handy-work.

Oh my god!
Shock, horror, the worst of all nightmare scenarios was staring back at me. I had the blackest of black, thick, exaggerated, caterpillar-looking brows you can imagine. Groucho Marx, to those who know of him,

eat your heart out. I virtually screamed at the perpetrator of this dire catastrophe that I couldn't walk out of the salon looking like that! How on earth had she managed to mutilate my brows when I had stressed the word 'natural'? Was she deaf? Did she have a hate thing for obronis or what?

My mind flashed to the comments and looks friends, work colleagues and, let's face it, strangers would give me if I were to step out looking like I had two thick black moustaches over my eyes. To say I was distraught was a gross understatement: I was mortified. Appreciating my slight concern, the masculine beautician, who appeared quite surprised at my reaction, acquired some cotton wool and what I truly believe to be nail varnish remover, and started to scrub and polish my eyebrows in a vain attempt to tone down 'the look'. All her efforts made little impact. The two black caterpillars were still staring back at me. She rubbed some more until my eyebrows began to feel sore. She said the dye was not permanent but I knew better. I reluctantly paid, believe it or not, for the Groucho Marx look, although I think I deducted a couple of cedis, and walked out of the salon, never to return.

To this day I swear my eyebrows owe their colour to the 'treatment' I had at the hands of an overzealous beautician working in Accra Mall.

Osu: The Oxford Street of Accra

Osu is a district in central Accra known for its busy commercial, restaurant and nightlife activity. The area has a buzz about it. The main road through Osu is Cantonments Road but it's colloquially known as Oxford Street – You can draw your own parallels. Osu is also the location of a shop called Global Mamas which all the volunteers visited at some time or other and the hospital I went to. (More later.) It was in Osu on one of my earliest visits, that I had my first successful experience of bartering when I bought a carved wooden box containing beads used to play the African game of Oware.

The main 'Oxford' street through Osu is accessed off a major roundabout/landmark called Danquah Circle. From Danquah it was possible to walk to the VSO Ghana office in Labone and so it was a location I visited quite often.

Osu is a popular area with tourists visiting Accra (and crafts are priced accordingly!).

Oxford Road itself was lined with street sellers touting their crafts for sale. Wood carvings, beaded jewellery, leather goods, dresses and prints/paintings were available in most of the roadside stores. The street traders were often pushy, but friendly enough and their prices were high but always subject to negotiation.

The district is famous for the Papaye, a restaurant known for its fast food and value, Frankie's - best known for its ice cream desserts and Container, a popular spot directly opposite Papaye with its Azonto music and buzzing atmosphere. It's a sit-out bar and eatery joint and at the weekends especially, there's usually a live music and acrobatic show.

A street off Cantonments Road would take you to the Sunshine Salad bar, a restaurant that Samina introduced me to. My first visit was with Samina and Ellie, a volunteer based in Bolgatanga, in northern Ghana. The salads are out of this world and well worth a visit.

Global Mamas, an NGO managed and run store in Osu was a popular place for volunteers to visit because of the range of fair trade gifts and clothes it sold. The NGO, called 'Women in Progress' sells goods made mostly by women working in co-operatives and living in Ghana. The store is just off the main Oxford (or Cantonments) Road, near to Danquah Circle and behind 'Koala', an upmarket supermarket. It sells clothes for men, women and children made in lovely batik, tie-dye and prints. It also sold a range of creative gifts including jewellery, bags, home decorations, body butter and soaps made from shea.

An example of the creativity of the goods on sale at Global Mamas was the range of bags and purses made from discarded water bags. Small plastic bags containing 'pure' water were sold everywhere by street traders, usually from a huge bowl carried on the heads of women and young girls. More often than not, the empty water bags would be thrown away as rubbish and left to line the streets in Accra. You'd also see masses of them swirling around in trotro stations. The NGO had resourcefully used the discarded water bags to make purses, pencil cases, toilet and cosmetic bags and tablet cases. I bought a number of small purses and use one now for coins. It was such a creative use of a readily available waste product. Another nice touch was the fact that the name of the woman who made the garment for sale in the shop would be written on a tag inside the item of clothing.

Visit to Koforidua

I was looking forward to staying for a night with Rhys and Lizzie who lived in Kof. I was excited as the trip was my first of any distance outside of Accra. The plan was for me to travel to Kof early Saturday morning, stay the night, and return on Sunday.

There were a number of ways to get to Kof by trotros. The one I opted for seemed the most straightforward and meant taking a trotro to Madina market and from there, change and catch another to Kof. As I felt I knew Madina trotro station following my memorable first day in work experience, I decided on this route.

I reached Madina before 8.00am in the morning with no problem and was directed to the queue for the trotro to Kof. This was an ill-defined line of people waiting in the middle of the open space which was the trotro station. As with all trotro stations I'd visited, it was absolutely full of trotros, of course, as well as people and litter. This one sadly had, in addition, a huge loud speaker system in the centre which kept blaring out the same message. I'm not sure what the message was, as it was in Twi, but it was monotonous, continuous, and very loud – and before long I'd have happily cut the wires to the system had I known where they were. Either that or assaulted the guy who was shouting down the tannoy.

I'd been told that trotros to Kof from Madina were frequent and that it should be easy to get one. However, what no-one had advised or knew about, and I hadn't planned for, was the fact that there was a funeral in Kof that weekend. This meant that there were a huge number of people all travelling the same way as me. Gradually, the queue I was standing in grew longer and longer as we all waited in the growing heat of the morning for a trotro to arrive.

As trotros are quite small mini-buses, it soon became clear, as the queue was getting longer, that even when a trotro for Kof did materialise, it couldn't accommodate all the people waiting for it. As I feared, when a trotro pulled in bound for Kof, the queue of people completely disaggregated as the mass charged at the bus. It was mad and chaotic and felt like, no was a stampede. A couple of trotros bound for Kof came, filled up and went. After each, I was inching towards the front of the queue hoping I would get on the next one. By this time I'd been standing in the queue for about an hour and was becoming hotter and more agitated at the noise, heat and the wait. Also, there was a Ghanaian woman a few people behind me who I suspected would push her way to the front when the next trotro arrived. She kept edging forward, looking around, fidgeting and generally had a 'ready to lurch' look about her.

I was right. As a trotro pulled in, what had been the queue nearest to the bus surged forward en mass. The Ghanaian woman who was behind me managed to push her way onto the trotro in front of me to the particular annoyance of another younger Ghanaian woman who started to complain vociferously. It made no difference. In the melee, I became lodged in a huddle near the door of the trotro.

I decided that if I didn't manage to get onto this trotro I'd give up, when out of thin air, an arm and hand stretched out and grabbed me. It was as if it was the hand of God. The hand dragged me to one side and thrust me to the door at the front of the trotro where there were usually two or three seats next to the driver. To say it was a relief is a gross understatement. I felt I'd been saved. I even had what was considered to be one of the best seats, sitting at the front of an air-conditioned trotro. (It was arguably one of the most dangerous seats too as trotros rarely have seat belts – but this one did!) This was sheer luxury and I couldn't have been happier. I remember feeling a bit guilty that I'd been given the seat because I was an obroni but I suppose it was as good a way as any to pick one person from the crowd to get on to the last seat on the bus - and I had been waiting for what seemed like an eternity. By God's Grace is the phrase that comes to mind.

The journey to Kof was my first experience travelling for any distance on a trotro out of Accra and it proved to be a positive one. The trotro was relatively new which, in my experience, was a rarity. The air conditioning made the journey much more comfortable and I enjoyed taking in the scenery. Climbing higher into the mountains, it became greener with more dense vegetation along the roadside beyond the red cliffs into which the road had been hewn. It was newly constructed and offered a smooth ride unlike the many potholed roads in Accra. Looking back afforded great views of the Accra plains and in the distance, the urban sprawl of Accra.

The journey took about three hours. It was immediately evident that the town was very different to Accra. The streets were more planned and it felt less busy. (I've just checked on Wikipedia where Koforidua is, to quote, *'regarded as one of the calmest and coolest cities in the country'*. So that concurs with my initial and subsequent impressions of the town.

I got off the trotro where I'd been advised and phoned the volunteers I was visiting. It didn't take long for Rhys to appear and we walked to their accommodation which was lovely and spacious. Lizzie was waiting to greet us there and was preparing lunch. Another volunteer, and friend, Vincent, was also visiting. He'd travelled from Asamankase where he was based. He was a lovely, gentle man, retired from working for local government and on his second VSO placement having lived and worked in India through VSO for two years. (I remember Vincent generously allowing me to use the only spare bed in the flat for our overnight stay which was gallant of him. I hope the settee he slept on wasn't too uncomfortable.)

So after lunch, the four of us planned what we'd do for the rest of the day. It was agreed that we'd go to Kof market which, although similar to the open markets in Accra, seemed more ordered and easier to walk through. The market sold everything from food to cooking utensils to clothes. I can remember buying a huge wooden spoon and a rustic mortar and pestle. I also bought a second-hand blouse for a pittance and a skirt. Kof is renowned for its bead market as the beads used for jewellery are made locally. Unfortunately the bead market was only there on Thursdays so I missed out. However, I did buy a bead bracelet from a small stall selling a range of jewellery to remind me of my visit. The bracelet was made of small (about half an inch long), pale blue, green, cream and grey tube shaped stones. Each bead had a thin stripe of cream, black, brown and yellow running around it. The beads have a tiny hole running through the centre and are threaded onto thin elastic to enable them to stretch easily over your hand and sit neatly on your wrist. Bead bracelets and necklaces are common in Ghana and come in all colours and sizes.

In the late afternoon we sat in a spot and enjoyed a cold drink (I had a Star, of course!) taking in views of the rooftops, streets and hills in the distance. We sat at tables on the first floor overlooking part of Kof where funeral ceremonies were taking place. No doubt many of those in attendance had been queuing in Madina with me. We all agreed that Kof was a pleasant contrast to Accra and much more peaceful. The evening was spent eating out at another local spot, chatting and chilling. It was a basic place with simple table and chairs where the locals ate so the food was known to be good. I had red red which was one of my favourite Ghanaian dishes.

I returned to Accra the following day having had one of the most pleasant weekends I can recall during my time in Ghana.

The Adabraka incident

Sitting quietly in Adabraka Cathedral, an imposing building in the middle of Accra with intricate masonry and stained glass windows, I was blissfully unaware of how the next three hours would unfold. I had no plans for them. But the innocent looking stranger who approached me had.

He'd followed me into the cathedral and we'd even exchanged a few words as we both wandered around the outside wondering where the main entrance was. It happened to be at the side of the cathedral. However, once inside the cavernous and beautiful building, we went our separate ways. I'd just had a meeting in central Accra with the Director of Ghana National Federation for the Disabled (GNFD) and had passed the cathedral as it was just across the road from where I was going. I decided then that I'd go in when I'd finished at GNFD. The rain fell as I emerged from my meeting so that provided a further impetus to go into the cathedral to shelter and be safe, or so I thought at the time.

I remember feeling reflective as I sat in a pew, lost in thought, but when I lifted my head, the stranger who'd entered the cathedral with me was standing next to me looking very agitated. He apologised instantly for interrupting me and his humble and apparent fragile state made me feel sorry for him. He immediately gained both my interest and sympathy. If only I'd been more circumspect and cynical at that stage. I should have known better.

So, this was the ruse: he said he was a diabetic and in desperate need of insulin. He'd taken a taxi to Accra airport in the morning for what he thought was an 11.00am flight home to Senegal. He'd been in Accra on business for the mining company he worked for and was returning to his expectant wife and young son, only to find that he'd got the flight time wrong. It left at 11.00pm that night. In view of the wait he'd have at the airport, he'd taken a taxi back to central Accra and had left his bag which contained his medication (insulin) and about $800 in the taxi in Kaneshie. He said he desperately needed an insulin shot and could I help, not to give money, but to accompany him to get the insulin. He said he'd already been to a pharmacist that could provide the medication he needed but they'd said he had to pay 970 Ghana cedis (about £300) to get a whole package containing a syringe and other necessary equipment, although he only needed insulin as he had a needle in another bag. He said his blood sugar level was getting high and he felt very ill, and to be honest, he looked it.

Now, in hindsight and in the cool light of day, 970 Ghana cedis or £300 UK equivalence, for whatever package of medication he needed sounds ridiculous but this was Ghana and things were different there. But what was I thinking? Well the question is probably better posed as, why wasn't I thinking? The answer was I wasn't thinking logically at all. I was simply re-acting to what I considered to be a potentially life-threatening situation for someone in need of help. We walked out of the cathedral together and initially sought advice from a nun who happened to be in the grounds. He explained his condition to her and asked where we might locate other pharmacies in the area. We were able to walk to one nearby but it didn't have what he needed. A woman in the pharmacy kindly phoned other chemists trying unsuccessfully to locate the insulin he claimed he needed. He told me he would be returning to the city, on business again, in a month.

From that pharmacy, we took a taxi and called at two others trying to source the insulin. All the time we were in the taxi, he kept thanking me and saying he didn't know how he would have managed without my help and company. He even showed me paperwork with information on it about his medical condition. Lots of hooks there I suppose. In desperation, we eventually called into a clinic where he insisted that he be given a blood sugar test. I actually saw him take the test, giving blood from his finger. He again pleaded for a particular type of insulin but the nurses at the clinic said they couldn't prescribe it. As time passed, the guy looked and acted more and more anxious and stressed.

For most of the time, I was not thinking about money or the cost of insulin or the package he'd alluded to. I just felt an overwhelming urge to help this man as he struggled to get his medication. The blood sugar test he took showed that it was high. He pressed the staff at the clinic and managed to see a doctor there. Again, I accompanied him. They had a discussion about what he needed and the doctor gave him a prescription for two different types of insulin and told him to go to a particular pharmacist to get it in an area called Asylum Down. I don't know why I didn't simply leave the doctor or clinic to sort out the problem. I wish I had. It felt bizarrely as though I was getting more and more deeply hooked, more and more deeply involved with this stranger and I couldn't tear myself away. I couldn't think of an excuse to leave him. It was as if I needed to resolve the dilemma. I wasn't, but I felt responsible.

We got back into the taxi which had been waiting for us and went to the pharmacy in Asylum Down. The guy spoke to the pharmacist who gave him some medication and I actually watched him inject himself in the stomach. He did this in front of me and other people who were waiting. However, he claimed that the other type of insulin he needed, the second part of the prescription, wasn't available. I personally checked this claim out with the pharmacist who confirmed that he'd run out of the second form of insulin which was on the prescription. The man paid for what he'd injected himself with. He said it made him feel better instantly and he acted in a more positive and upbeat manner. Why didn't I leave him then? Again I have no answer although by this time, I know for sure that I wanted to. I'd been with this stranger for far too long and wanted to escape but something inside me now felt tied to him. It felt as though I was being reeled in ever more slowly but tightly into a thickening plot which was getting murkier by the minute.

We got back into the same taxi to go in search of the second part of the prescription. At this juncture, as he'd said he couldn't afford the second prescription, I suggested that we go to Adabraka police station to get help. Something inside me felt the need to test the legitimacy of this man and if he needed help, the local police station seemed to be the obvious place to find it and to test out his story. It was beginning to feel like a macabre game, and I was playing it out with him. Would I be able to catch him out? He was quite happy to go to the police station, so we went and after a confused wait, (Ghanaian police stations are not the most savoury places to hang out in) he actually told a senior police officer his whole story. As the lack of money to secure the insulin he needed now seemed to be his prime focus of concern, the officer just dismissed the case and said he couldn't help. He said the loss of his bag in the taxi should have been reported at the local police station in Kaneshie. So we left.

If the police wouldn't help, why did I feel the need to continue to do so? It's difficult to explain and I showed poor judgement at the time. However, I was fully aware that this was Ghana and things and people don't work in quite the same way as they do in the UK. After the visit to the police station, the conversation and concern changed focus to that of money and his inability to pay for the prescription he claimed he needed. He said he would pay me back for any money I lent him.

At this point in the scam, in hindsight, I wish I'd not had my debit cards with me. If this had been the case, I wouldn't have been in a position to give him any money in the first place. This was the cruel twist of fate, the irony of the situation which seemed lost on me at the time. I told him I didn't have a bank account in Ghana so he couldn't pay me back. But he had an answer. He then took me to the Western Credit Union bank which confirmed that he could transfer money to me without me having an account there. He seemed to bat everything back that I threw at him and by now it was feeling impossible to get away. I was not only hooked but was being slowly reeled in. I'd stayed with him for too long and I'd missed my chances to escape. But I knew in my gut that it didn't feel right.

We left the Western Credit Union bank and he now insisted he needed money to go back to the pharmacy he'd been to before we met. He said he'd need to pay the 970 Ghana cedis to get the package containing the insulin he needed. So I caved in, and we went to a bank where I withdrew the maximum amount my debit card would allow, which was 400 Ghana cedis. (About £130.)

We went back to the cathedral where we exchanged personal information and I handed him the money. He wrote a name, phone number, email address and his work organisation on a piece of paper and I gave him my details. He then said he would try to get back to the pharmacy he'd contacted first and as we left the cathedral for a second time, I even asked a man in a 4x4 who was waiting in the grounds if he could take us to another cash point to try to get more money for him. I withdrew another 200 Ghana cedis and, zombie-like, gave it away.

His final coup came when he suggested, as he claimed he still didn't have all the money he needed, it would be better if he went on a trotro to the pharmacy alone. The reason he gave for this was that if he was seen with a white person the pharmacist would expect him to be able to borrow all the money for the prescription from me and he wouldn't be given the medication for the 600 Ghana cedis I'd given him. I think we were both tiring of the charade by this stage. Before leaving him I asked if he would mind if I took his photo. This was to be my trump card. With total effrontery, he posed for me. He said he'd contact me within an hour to confirm that he'd got the insulin and before he left I asked him not to let me down in terms of returning the money I had given him, not to destroy my faith in human nature.

I never heard from him again.

Epilogue

I was so distraught and embarrassed by my own gullibility that I went to see a fellow volunteer to confide. She said I shouldn't blame myself or feel gullible and that I was only drawn in because I was so caring. She couldn't believe the lengths he went to to convince me. She was sympathetic and that helped. I will never forget her kind words and her generosity in supporting me at that time.

A week or so later, I told my story to Awo and staff at GNECC who insisted I report the incident to the police at Adabraka police station. There's a bitter irony there don't you think? I also told VSO Ghana.

It's a long story, but, in brief, I made my statement. As the station didn't have the facility to download the photo from my camera that I'd taken of the scammer, an off-duty officer took me on the back of his motorbike, and no, we weren't wearing crash helmets, to a local place where they printed copies. This was Ghana remember. I left all the details at the police station but they never got back to me. Later still, I shared the photo with other volunteers, one of whom put it on Facebook.

I then learned that other volunteers had been approached by the scammer in Ghana and in adjacent African countries using the same storyline. He even tried the same scam on Waqas who, at that time, had only recently joined GNECC!

It seems he's still operating out there so be warned.

Visit to Akosombo Dam and Lake Volta, 26th May 2012

The Volta Region is the most easterly region in Ghana and shares a border with Togo. It's dominated by Lake Volta and is known as one of the most beautiful areas in the country. We were heading for the town of Akosombo, about 85km north of Accra in the Volta Region where you can see the dam which has created Lake Volta, the largest man-made lake in Africa. The hydro-electric dam generates enough power to service Ghana as well as supplementing the power requirements of neighbouring countries such as Togo, Benin, and the Ivory Coast.

Akosombo is the town established when the dam was built. The project resulted in the dispersion of thousands of local Ghanaians and 28 people working on the construction project were killed in the process. To travel to Akosombo, we needed to get to the bus station at Tudu which is an area in downtown Accra near the coast. It's also the location of a huge market. From the bus station we'd be able to catch a trotro direct to Akosombo. To make the most of the day, we needed an early start so I was up and out of the flat well before 6.00am travelling on a trotro headed for Tudu.

Ghanaians never seem to sleep or appear to need very little. They are up at the break of dawn in the morning (to make the most of the cooler temperatures) and stay up late into the night. So it was not surprising that Tudu was a hive of activity by the time we got there with people setting up their stalls or moving goods around on carts. It was teeming with people preparing for the day ahead and there was a bustle about the place.

As I sat in the packed trotro which took us to Tudu, I remember checking my Nokia phone which I always kept in an embroidered pouch in the front zipped pocket of my yellow rucksack. I'd also put about 300 cedis (about £100) in the pouch with the phone. As we got off the trotro, I was following a Ghanaian friend, Kwame, who was accompanying me to the dam. He went on ahead and, in the throng of people, I remember it being quite difficult to keep up with him. I was constantly on the move dodging and weaving between and amongst people with my rucksack bobbing up and down on my back.

We reached the stand in the bus station where we had to pay for the tickets and I shuffled off my rucksack to find my money and pay. As I looked in the front of my rucksack, I can't recall whether it was zipped or unzipped. All I can remember vividly is the sinking feeling in the pit of my stomach as I realised my purse, which contained my mobile phone and money, was not where it normally was, where I always left it. I rummaged through the rest of my rucksack, frantically moving every item whilst, deep down, knowing it had gone.

My heart raced, stomach churned, and I felt sick as I realised someone had stolen both my money and phone. A mix of emotions followed ranging from disbelief that someone had managed to unzip my rucksack without me feeling it, to amazement that I'd been robbed whilst I was almost running along and a sadness that in the crowded streets, no-one had warned me or tried to stop the thief. People must have seen the theft. I was beyond gutted.

We retraced our steps back through the crowded streets and my companion used his phone to call my stolen mobile. It rang but we couldn't hear it, and then it stopped ringing. It went dead. We were powerless and had to let it go, although in the moment it was hard to give it up. We needed to decide whether to continue with our plan to visit Akosombo. We decided not to let the event spoil our day and, fortunately, I'd enough money located elsewhere in my rucksack for the trotro journey and so we went.

It was difficult to get the theft out of my head as the trotro travelled north out of Accra. The phone had been given to me as a gift just before I went to Kenya. The purse also contained my VSO permit, a considerable amount of money, and some medication. But there was no option; I had to let it go. Despite knowing this fact, I was totally in my head for most of the journey to our destination and more or less oblivious to the scenery en route.

Akosombo was a beautiful place and so well worth visiting. We met some locals who helped us to secure a conducted tour of the power generating station. I'll never forget the noise of the turbines as we ventured below ground to witness all the workings of the station and learn about the constant monitoring that goes on around the clock. The scale of the equipment used to control and monitor the workings of dam is incredible with a massive underground network of machinery, screens and electrical gadgetry as well as staff to help to do so.

Outside, the dam itself is the most amazing piece of engineering. Behind a monstrous wall of grey concrete, (660 metres (2,165.33 ft.) long, 114 metres (374 ft.) high and 366 meters (1,200.77ft) wide at base) it holds back a huge expanse of water. It is a truly monumental piece of engineering.

The town of Akosombo itself is so different to Accra. It was originally built to house the people working on the dam. It was quiet, orderly and well planned and has an air of peace and calm. There were fewer people and the pace of life appeared slower.

Lake Volta is the world's largest artificially created lake. It is an expansive mass of glistening water which goes on and on as far as the eye can see and beyond, covering an area of 8,502 square kilometres. It has a maximum length of 400km (250 miles!) and a shoreline of 7,250 km-not that I walked around it to confirm! It is vast. The lake stretches from the dam which blocked the river Volta to Yapei in the north. It is surrounded by mountains, rolling hills, valleys and rocky outcrops covered by rich vegetation sweeping down to the shore. The scale of it makes the Lake District Finger Lakes seem small in comparison but it does have a look of the Lakes but on a much, much grander scale.

Although the original idea for the dam dates back to 1915, it was not until 1949 that plans began to be drawn up and finally executed in 1961. It was completed in 1965. As a newly independent country,

Ghana wanted to expand the economy by way of industrial development and so the final proposal outlined the building of an aluminium smelter at Tema, a dam constructed at Akosombo to power the smelter, and a network of power lines installed through southern Ghana.

The creation of the lake resulted in the flooding of 15,000 homes and of 740 villages and the resettlement of 78,000 people. The lake is navigable and provides a cheap route linking Ghana's northern savanna with the coast. It is also a major fishing ground and provides irrigation water for farmland in the dry Accra Plains lying immediately below the dam site. The generating capacity of the dam's hydroelectric power plant is 912 megawatts of electricity.

On our return journey, we stopped just south of Akosombo to see the famous Adomi Bridge which spans the Volta River at the village of Atimpoku. It's a two-hinged steel arch bridge with a deck suspended by cables (for lovers of bridges and detail). Its arched structure which has a crisscross pattern of supporting steel cables makes it look like a beautifully symmetrical steel rainbow. We walked across the bridge and took photos of the river, the fishermen, and the surrounding hills which were covered in a carpet of green and tried not to get run over by the traffic as we gazed at the bridge and the views from it.

The trip to Akosombo dam was memorable for many reasons. With time, the memory of the theft has diminished, whilst the memory of the beauty of

Lake Volta and Akosombo remains strong.

'One Day' – a poem for my Ghanaian friend Kwame

Start of the week, pick car early for work,
pay's kakra kakra but that's how
it is for now, somehow.

With work all day and school at night
I'm managing,
one day.

Feet carry me through the next five days,
I'm weary with this long 'ole road,
but I know the end's in sight, all right.

With work all day and school at night,
I'm managing,
one day 'o'.

Chat with the ladies, date small okay,
no plan to commit just yet at all,
just coping with how things are, so far.

With work all day and school at night,
I'm managing,
one day.

Check out Facebook, WhatsApp an' all,
step out, drink beer, smoke small
to keep me sane, no blame.

With work all day and school at night,
I'm managing,
one day 'o'.

Thank God for Friday, best day of the week,
meet up, play snooker
stay out late, to celebrate.

With work all day and school at night,
I'm managing,
one day.

Saturday breathe free, sleep sound and long,
hand washing now, if the water's on.
Enjoy the day, that's my way.

With work all day and school at night,
I'm managing,
one day 'o'.

Church on Sunday to pay my dues,
look down on me Lord and keep me strong.
Got my goal, it's in my soul.

With work all day and school at night,
I'm managing,
one day.

Collect the cards and network well
for now and in the future,
all will be good, as it should.

With work all day and school at night,
I'm managing,
one day 'o'.

My day will come, wife, kids, good job,
it will all be worthwhile and I'll smile,
'til then.

With work all day and school at night,
I'm managing,
life is sweet 'o'.

Visit to the hospital

I'd tried everything I, and the local pharmacist, thought might work to get rid of the rash I developed at the back of my legs and lower part of my bum. It was unpleasant, red and sore. I'd tried washing regularly, talcum powder, an antiseptic cream and a special talcum powder which was supposed to be anti-fungal, the latter recommended by the pharmacist in Roman Ridge. Nothing was touching it and it seemed to be getting worse.

In relation to the possible cause of the problem, I felt it might be prickly heat exacerbated by the fact that I was sitting down in the office at GNECC for much of the day. I was certainly hot and sweaty for most of the time unless the air conditioning was full on. (I even used to put my arms into the deep freeze compartment of the fridge-freezer in the kitchen at GNECC in an effort to try to cool down, much to the amusement of the occasional member of staff who caught me!) Also, one of the side effects of the anti-malarial tablets I was taking was skin disorders.

As my home treatments were having no impact, I decided a trip to the hospital was in order.

I went to The Trust hospital in Osu, signed various forms at the reception desk giving VSO Ghana as my address and was told to sit down in a waiting area along with what appeared to be an endless queue of Ghanaians. I waited and waited, and waited, and waited. It was tiring and hot. People seemed to be called in no particular order but I'm sure there was a system. It was just the waiting and not knowing when you would be seen that made it a bit frustrating.

About an hour and a half later, I saw a female doctor. She looked at my skin problem and confirmed it was infected. I'd wondered whether the anti-malarial tablets I was taking could have contributed to the skin condition and mentioned this to the doctor. She wasn't sure but felt it was a possibility. I had an interesting conversation with her about taking anti-malarial tablets, which don't by the way, actually stop you from catching malaria but apparently ameliorate the symptoms if you do get it. She was sure that during the five months that I'd been in Ghana I would have built up a natural immunity and so didn't need to continue taking any tablets. She was adamant on this subject.

The medical team at VSO (London based) held, and I'm sure still hold, an equally strong opposing view. They responded promptly to an email I sent about the Ghanaian doctor's opinion by re-affirming the need to continue taking anti-malarial tablets whilst I was in Ghana.

I took the prescription I was given for my skin issue to the pharmacy based at the hospital and waited for my treatments. Thankfully a much shorter wait. These included anti-biotic tablets, anti-biotic cream and a disinfectant wash which I had to dilute in water and sit in on a daily basis. I suppose I hadn't thought too long or hard about the quality of the water I was using in the flat to wash and shower although I certainly knew you couldn't drink it. I just didn't think about how unclean it was. Evidence of its poor quality was the fact that I remember leaving a cup of water in the kitchen at GNECC over one weekend and when I returned to work on the Monday morning, the water looked and smelled decidedly unpleasant with green fungal gunge on it! So I was washing in poor quality water from my shower and sink on a daily basis as we had no hot water. (I'm sure this didn't cause my skin infection but it certainly didn't help to cure it!)

The doctor advised me to put the wash in my bath and seemed surprised when I told her I didn't have one. Clearly it would appear that most obronis are expected to live in more up market accommodation than mine. So, with no bath to soak in, I had to fill a plastic bowl with some hot water I'd boiled each morning, add some of the disinfectant/wash to it and sit in it for about five minutes! I must have looked a sight, but needs must!

Thankfully, the treatment did the trick and within a few weeks, the rash started to fade.

I was asked to return to the hospital to check how the medication was working and saw another female doctor about a month later who was happy with the improvement.

I was lucky that a relatively minor skin infection was the only real health problem I had whilst I was in Ghana, together with a number of mosquito bites, all, thankfully, by the male variety of the species! Other volunteers were not so fortunate and at least four that I knew developed malaria. The stories which circulated amongst the volunteers about the symptoms they had and conditions in the hospitals where they were treated (mainly in the north of Ghana) were horrific. There were tales of claw hands, extreme sickness and lethargy. The conditions they experienced in hospital were equally scary and included being injected using blunt needles, dirty bed linen and not being provided with any food or facilities to wash. It sounded grim. Volunteers who did contract malaria were, in the main, brought down to Accra for treatment and to recover.

You're strongly advised to take anti-malarial medication if you go to Ghana as it's high risk throughout the country. I started out taking doxycycline and then, following my skin issue, requested that VSO change my prescription to Malarone which supposedly has fewer side effects. They agreed to my request and on a positive note, my skin problem didn't recur.

Trip to the Wii Falls and the Monkey Sanctuary in the Volta Region

I hadn't done a great deal of travelling around Ghana, mainly due to the poor roads and poor quality, albeit cheap, means of transport, by which I mean trotros. I was also, for the most part, happy to simply 'be' in Accra. However, a new volunteer with GNECC, Waqas, was planning to go to the northern part of the Volta region, which was an area I wanted to explore further. I had, of course visited Akosombo and Lake Volta in the southern part of the region. It's renowned for being green and lush and it also has the highest mountain areas in the country, the highest peak being Mount Afadja at a height of 885 metres (2,904 ft.) which is located in the Agumatsa Range.

So, after some hesitation and indecision, I managed to get myself up at 4.30am on a Saturday morning and got down to the bus station in Tudu where the trotro to Hohoe, our initial destination, was due to leave and where we'd agreed to meet. This was the area where I'd had my phone and money stolen the last time I went travelling but fortunately there were no disasters this time!

I was misinformed about the means of transport we were planning to use as we thought there would be an air conditioned bus; however, that wasn't the case for whatever reason on Saturdays, so it was a four and half hour trotro ride to our first stop at Kpandu. Again for some reason there were no trotros to Hohoe that day so we had to take a detour. I swear trotros don't have springs or shock absorbers and the seats on the trotros have little padding due to wear and tear. On a Saturday morning, driving along potholed roads, I fully appreciated why I'd not done much travelling before!

From Kpandu we took a shared taxi to Hohoe and from there negotiated with the driver to take us to the Wii falls which are the highest waterfalls in West Africa. The fall is majestic in scale with the gushing white water of the Agumatsa River thundering about 60 meters down steep cliffs into a large pool below. It was a 40 minute walk through luxurious forest along a well-worn path to the falls (of course you had to pay to see the falls). It was peaceful and quite spiritual to walk along the river taking in the different environment. The rich variety of vegetation combined with the sporadic bursts of light produced every shade of green you can imagine with the sunlight streaking through gaps in the foliage and reflecting the contrasting colours. There were so many different varieties of trees and plants, some with massive leaves, others creeping around and dangling from higher species. The overall form of the plants and trees created several distinct layers typical of tropical forest.

The height of the Wii falls generated lots of spray and there were masses of bats milling around the rocks on either side of the falls. The combination of water and sunlight on that day produced a near perfect rainbow near the base of the waterfall. The arc of rainbow colours at the base of the falls shimmered opaquely against the white spray of the cascading water. While lots of Ghanaians splashed around in the water at the base of the falls fully clothed and Waqas also took the plunge, I was quite content to paddle around the edge.

Walking back to the reception hut, we witnessed something quite extraordinary: along the path about 50 yards in front of us, we saw two black cobras mating. Ironically, we'd asked the guide who took us to the falls if there were any snakes around and he'd confidently said there weren't. As soon as he realised what was in front of us, he visibly panicked, raising his voice and motioning for us to retreat. He insisted we keep well back whilst he proceeded to throw rocks at the snakes.

Waqas naively asked if they were dancing and the guide confirmed they were *'having sex'*.

Being reckless, we wanted to get nearer to see the spectacle close up. Crazy I know. They were huge. You could see their long bodies and heads writhing first in one direction and then the other, one minute lengthening and then recoiling from one another, linking and intertwining their bodies together like twisted rope. It was a mating ritual which was being performed across the width of the footpath in front of our eyes. I managed to take some photos and a short video clip of the cobra although sadly they're rather dark. You can still make out the cobra though.
I have no idea how close I might have got to them before realising the danger had I been walking in front.

Following our eventful walk back from the falls, we chilled in a beautiful spot overlooking the mountains with an ice cold bottle of Star. After recovering from the cobra episode, we took motorbike rides back to Hohoe and stayed there for the night.

On Sunday morning we headed off for the famous monkey sanctuary at Tafi Atome village which is about 43 km south of Hohoe.

The monkeys there will feed directly from your hand. I'd been thinking about this before sleeping on Saturday night and was not at all sure about it but decided to *'go with the flow'*. We negotiated a trotro ride; it's amazing how trotros just seem to appear. The monkey sanctuary was another incredible experience. Again, we had to pay to be taken into the forest area by a young girl who was our guide. We bought bananas, as instructed, and after about a five minute walk, we arrived at a small clearing where she called for the monkeys on a strange instrument about the size of a mouth organ. The noise it made when she blew into it attracted the monkeys in an instant, although I can't recall the sound it made.

The monkeys, which I believe are a species called 'Mona', appeared from nowhere. They varied in size, the majority being small at about 12 to 14 inches. They all had mottled brown fur on their backs, as if they were wearing a coat. Their legs and extremely long thin tails were grey. They sported a white bib beneath a small head and the front of their bodies and inner part of their legs were white too. They appeared to be wearing a grey mask on their faces and around their bright beady eyes which were large, brown in colour with jet black pupils. They had tiny hands and feet with thin nimble fingers.

As soon as the girl handed us a banana from our small bag, a monkey would literally leap onto you, peel the banana at break neck speed whilst it was still in your hand and eat it. They were so dexterous and quick. Once the banana was eaten they'd dart off in a millisecond. My heart was pounding the whole time but it was an amazing experience to feel the weight of their bodies pounce onto you, perfectly poised, and to feel them gently clinging to your arm, hand or shoulder.

I have a great photo of a monkey sitting squarely on my shoulder, bum nestled in my neck and long tail resting down my chest like a pigtail. I, in contrast, look less than comfortable.

I gather we were lucky that none of them had a wee on us which is quite common and wouldn't have been so pleasant! I'd not thought about that possibility beforehand though. I had asked another guide whether or not anyone had ever been bitten by a monkey and he reliably informed me not, but there's always a first time, and we'd been told there were no black cobras in the forest walking to the Wii falls!

Apparently the monkeys are considered to be sacred and believed to have some spiritual powers. For this reason, the people of Tafi have been protecting them for the past 200 years and tradition doesn't allow them to be killed or harmed.

I wished we'd had more bananas but we were only allowed to buy a few to enable other visitors to feed them. We took lots of photos and I'm sure those of me show the fear in my eyes but I was pleased I'd had the courage to stand my ground in the clearing and feed the 'special' monkeys.

We looked around the village adjacent to the sanctuary and I took a photo of some children drawing water from a bore hole. So many of the children you see have so little and are so poor and yet they are nearly always smiling, warm and friendly as they call out to you. We took another trotro back to Ho and yet another to the small village of Atimpoku (location of the Adomi Bridge) on the river near Akasombo where the dam at Volta Lake is located. We had a bite to eat in Atimpoku before catching a trotro back to Accra.

Arriving in Accra at about 6.30pm, I felt I'd been to the far reaches of northern Ghana and back but, if you look on a map of Ghana, I'd barely travelled any distance north as the Wii falls are only about 223 km north east of Accra.

I'd nevertheless had a wonderful time and probably enjoyed it all the more for not having done much travelling before.

(For comparison, the total straight line distance between Accra and Navrongo on the border between Ghana and Burkina Faso in the north is just over 600 km or 373.4 miles.)

Trip to Lome, the capital of Togo

It was all arranged at the very last minute. I was sitting having a Star in a spot called 'The Living Room' in East Legon after work on Friday with Waqas who I'd visited the Volta Region with when visiting Togo was raised and discussed. We decided to go the next day.

It meant another early start from Tudu but, after some uncertainty about which trotro to catch and a short wait, we got on one bound for the border where we would cross into Togo. The journey took us through villages and more open countryside I'd not seen before and latterly along the coast. We were heading due east. The trotro stopped a couple of times to enable passengers to buy street food and drink and the time passed quickly.

Once at the border town of Aflao on the Ghanaian side, we had to get through customs or border control. If my life depended on it, I couldn't explain the process we went through. We seemed to be checked at a number of stages, showing passports and being asked questions and then moving to another room or building. I do remember feeling hard done by because Waqas, who obviously had a Canadian passport, paid far less than I did to get through the border control. I couldn't see the fairness or logic in that. I think the amount someone pays is probably a variable feast but I eventually got my passport stamped with an elaborate stamp and we walked into Togo. Once across the border we were stopped again and our belongings checked, presumably for drugs. After questioning and bag searches, we were both deemed to be 'clean' and allowed to continue. At this stage, neither of us had any Togo currency so we needed to sort that out. There were plenty of 'dealers' milling around prepared to offer what they said was the best price for exchanging money.

Unlike Accra, one of the most popular means of transport in Lome, which is the capital city of Togo and directly across the border on the coast, was by motorcycle. We each hailed a bike and agreed a fare to take us to the centre of Lome where we hoped to see the main attractions. Lome is renowned for having a palm-lined and expansive stretch of sandy beach which, I have to admit, did provide a stunning backdrop to the capital city. It also has a beautiful cathedral which dominates the city centre.

We walked around Lome and spent some time in the outdoor market which was quite similar to the busy markets in Accra with all the hustle, bustle, colour and vibrancy. There was the same freneticism and lots of huge colourful umbrellas shading the traders from the sun. These looked particularly colourful from the elevated positions afforded by the balconies in the indoor market. What was strange was the fact that everyone was now speaking in French. Just one step across the border and the national language changed from English to French. We also wandered around the huge indoor market hall which was located in a rambling old building on three levels and is known as Lome Grand Market. We found a spot where we could drink and eat. It was pretty basic but I remember the bread was delicious, just like soft French baguettes. Lome has a reputation for having some good restaurants and tea and coffee were sold in the street which was very different to Accra which had few places offering hot refreshments at all.

In the afternoon Waqas decided to visit the famous - or infamous - fetish market place which sold voodoo (related to the West African religion) and all things related to Ju-Ju (objects, such as amulets, and spells used in religious practices, as part of witchcraft in West Africa). It was some way out of the centre of Lome. I decided not to pay the entrance fee and visit but I could see some of the goods on display from the roadside – skulls, bones, masks and weird looking dolls were laid out on tables in a large outdoor space but there was also an indoor aspect to the market which, of course, I didn't have access to. I was told that on entry, you were offered a talk about voodoo and the potential benefits to be gained from certain gadgets and potions. The emphasis was, apparently, on fertility and all things sexual. It made me think of Viagra and oysters. My cynical view on this is if they really worked, those owning the market would be multi-millionaires.

We had a meal in the evening and took in the Lome night scene which I didn't find particularly impressive. It felt a bit like walking along the front at Blackpool in the height of the season with all the lights and noise but with the added factor of high humidity and heat. Maybe we just didn't know the 'in' places to go.

The following day, we walked along the huge expanse of fine sandy beach which provides the distinctive coastline at Lome. Most of the beach was deserted due to the vast area it covers. The sand was fine, completely free of rubbish and fringed nearest the road with coconut palms under which concrete benches had been randomly placed. People were sitting or lying under the trees with their distinctive feathery fronds sprouting from the top of their trunks- eating or sleeping. It was a balmy scene.

We headed back to Accra in the early afternoon. I did enjoy the trip to Lome and it was interesting to visit another African country, but I was not as impressed with my trip to Togo as I had been with our trip to the Volta Region in Ghana.

The tick incident

It makes my skin crawl and I get goose bumps remembering this bizarre incident but it happened at dusk as I was walking from Kotoka Airport. I remember the light fading and the air being sticky and humid.

I decided to go to the airport to say good-bye to a young Canadian volunteer, Helen, (not from VSO but from WUSC) who'd been working briefly for GNECC. She was only on a short, two month placement but had initially been based at the White House. She didn't find the transition from Canada to Ghana easy and had a fiancé back home who she missed a lot.

She'd been sent to Cape Coast to undertake some research on behalf of the GNECC but her placement, overall, didn't seem to go very well. There appeared to be an issue about finances at some point which proved a tricky one to deal with. We'd kept in touch via text but didn't know one another very well. Anyway, she was leaving and as no-one else I knew was going to see her off, I decided to go to Kotoka to do so. I think she was relieved to be leaving.

As I was walking from the airport along the scrub and tree-lined Airport road and before reaching Liberation road, something pricked the inside of my right wrist. I immediately felt the point where the sensation was and rubbed it. It felt as though there was a tiny pinhead beneath my skin. (I've actually got goose bumps as I write this.) The sensation developed into an irritation and I couldn't resist scratching the skin where the pinhead seemed to be embedded. I kept scratching and had no idea at the time what was causing the weird sensation in my wrist. It just felt odd and whatever it was I wanted it out from under my skin.

I kept walking and scratching until I thought that whatever it was had been literally dug out by my nails. The tiny lump seemed to have gone. Now I've had no experience of ticks. I'd been asked to check Mungo for them but was decidedly reluctant to do so and thankfully never found any on him. Apparently his ears were prone. I'd just never, to the best of my knowledge, been in contact with one of the little critters.

After walking for about 25 minutes, I reached Airport West where I was house and dog sitting at the time. I looked more closely in the light at my wrist and, not surprisingly, with all the scratching I'd done it was red and a bit sore. Later that evening, when my lower wrist and hand swelled and I began to be concerned, I checked on-line about ticks. For some reason I determined it must have been a tick that managed to lodge itself in my wrist but I've no idea where it came from. The information I read was neither pleasant nor encouraging. Apparently you have to be very careful removing ticks to ensure that no part of it is left in your body. The fact that my wrist and hand had swollen was a bit scary.

Fortunately, by the next day, the swelling appeared to have gone down and thankfully, as of today, I have no visible evidence of any skin invasion. Nevertheless, the memory of the incident and the short term scare it created still, as I said, makes my skin crawl.

I never did find out for definite that it was a tick, but I'm sure it was.

Ghanaian food

Ghanaian food is distinctive and memorable. Whether it's street food - which is readily available everywhere in Ghana - Ghanaian food served in a restaurant, or traditional home cooking, it's usually hot and spicy and always has lots of flavour. To produce the various Ghanaian dishes, red and green chillies are frequently used, together with spices such as thyme, garlic, ginger, curry, basil, nutmeg, sumbala and bay leaves. These are used in soups and stews. The food does take some getting used to though and I did lose weight during the first few months of my stay in the country.

    I was especially fortunate to have a colleague and friend, Awo, who was a superb cook and who used to bring me lunch most days in work. That was great as, although I enjoy good food, I can't claim to be an avid or committed cook. I have a tendency to pick at food and snack and rarely cook from scratch for myself. I do have a philosophy however that anyone who can read can cook; it just takes time, effort and inclination. There's something special in my mind though about someone who holds wonderful recipes in their head, can cook without a recipe book and is carrying on a cooking tradition handed down from mother to daughter. This would apply to Awo.

    Awo has amazing taste buds as well as culinary skills. She'd be able to tell by taste how old a fish was and had honed her skills to determine exactly how long to cook and simmer each stage of any

Ghanaian dish she was preparing. I did spend time watching her in her kitchen, but she was of the school which used a dash of this and a splodge of that, followed by lots of tasting, rather than meticulously weighing and measuring out quantities of ingredients, so whilst I got a rough idea of how to cook certain Ghanaian dishes, such as jollof rice and red red and even have a few notes to prove my intent, a couple of attempts to replicate these on my part didn't come near the standards reached so effortlessly by Awo. Okay, I acknowledge she'd had years of practice.

Sadly it seems, I'm of the Delia Smith School of cookery which requires all ingredients meticulously listed and weighed and the method outlined precisely to secure the desired outcome. (I once did cook a mean moussaka though following one of Delia's recipes!)

My favourites of Awo's Ghanaian dishes included red red and jollof rice. Awo's elder son, Darkeh who was six years old, shared my love of jollof.

Red red consists of red beans cooked in palm oil, which gives it its colour, onion, ginger, garlic and tomato sauce, usually served with spicy plantains (giant bananas). The plantains complement the red red perfectly but were incredibly filling. The trick was to know when you'd had sufficient. The dish was so moreish it was easy to eat too much and suffer later from a distended stomach (groan!). I just didn't want to stop eating. Jollof rice, or just 'jollof' as it was called, was another favourite and consisted of spicy flavoured rice (with tomatoes, tomato paste, onions, salt, cumin, nutmeg, ginger and chilli peppers), which was often served with chicken or another type of meat.

The staples of the Ghanaian diet are various starch-based, somewhat dough-like substances which included fufu, (made with a flour from the cassava plant - or alternatively another flour, such as semolina or maize flour), banku (fermented meal of maize or cassava or a combination of both- much like kenkey, but boiled directly in a pot), and kenkey (similar to a sourdough dumpling but wrapped in a foil, corn husk or plantain leaves).

Funnily enough I mistook kenkey for a form of fuel for quite a long time as it's wrapped in leaves. When I saw them stacked up I thought they were something you burned on a fire or stove to heat your home. (Given the heat in Ghana, I accept it was not a very logical thought.) Ah well, you live and learn.

Anyway, these starch based foods would normally be served with a variety of meat stews such as chicken, goat or an animal I'd never heard of before called a grasscutter. For a long time I thought this was some kind of grass hopper, or maybe I just misheard the name. It turns out that the creature (grasscutter) which looks distinctly like a rat with a long tail is bred and caught in Ghana. It was a meat I was never tempted to try and even less so when I saw the dead animals staked out in the market place where they looked distinctly rat like. Awo advised me that there were two ways to kill grasscutter and she was only inclined to consider eating those killed in a trap. She was of the view that those killed by shotgun could result in lead poisoning in humans from the bullets.

You would always know when fufu was being prepared as the process of preparation involved a lengthy and monotonous pounding of the maize using a long and very heavy pole in what was basically a giant mortar and pestle. You would regularly hear the thud, thud, thud of fufu being pounded in preparation for an evening meal. I did have a go at pounding the stuff once and believe me, you needn't go to the gym to develop your biceps if you pounded fufu regularly enough!

Banku was another starch-based product eaten with stew and often with a fish called tilapia, a fish with a white, fine textured meat and a very mild flavour. They typically have deep compressed bodies and look a bit like haddock or a sea bass only with deeper bodies. They often have a long dorsal (along the back) fin, and a lateral line (along the side) which often breaks towards the end of the dorsal fin, and starts again two or three rows of scales below. I can definitely vouch for the fact that tilapia have strong dorsal fins as I once sat with Awo in her kitchen cutting the fins off tilapia which a friend had bought from a tilapia farm. A smelly, but not unpleasant business. It amused Awo to watch me. Tilapias are often sold dried. In this form, they look flat and very salty. I never sampled the fish in this state.

Of course Awo knew all the best places to buy tilapia if it was purchased off the street.

Awo also prepared a couscous type of food called gari which was usually eaten with hard boiled eggs and was commonly accompanied, as with many dishes, by a hot and very spicy sauce called shito. When eating out, Awo would advise me on the strength of the shito she felt my pallet would tolerate. There are some really powerful shito sauces out there, believe me, which could easily blow your head off. So, I was fortunate indeed to have sampled an amazing variety of high quality Ghanaian home cooking courtesy of my friend and colleague Awo for which I will be eternally grateful.

As I said, Ghana has a huge variety of street food which varies according to the time of day. Early in the morning, a grey sort of gruel was widely on offer served up, if desired, with a fried fritter type of dough. I have to confess the grey gruel was a dish I never sampled or wished to, but it was very popular with Ghanaians. If not eaten in the makeshift roadside cafes, the grey runny substance would be spooned into a plastic bag and taken away to consume, off-site.

Also popular with morning consumers was a dish called watchi. This is another rice based dish made from black-eyed peas and rice which again, I was never particularly tempted by although a number of colleagues used to bring this into GNECC and sit to eat it in the kitchen before starting work. A particular favourite with a young colleague, Katie, the young volunteer from Canada was a large, sweet doughnut ball. These would be fried in huge cauldron-like pans on a fire in the open air and the aroma reminded me of the sickly sweet smell of fun fares and candyfloss back in the UK.

Later in the day the street food on offer would change as roasted plantains might be available or a great delicacy called kelewele, which was the street name given to spicy plantains. Other street foods included roasted corn on the cob, hard boiled eggs offered with shito sauce (which I really enjoyed as a snack) and fried plantains, which made wonderful thick wedge shaped chips, also served with shito.

Most spots sold food or had a street seller next to them offering cooked food. More often than not they would sell kebabs of either goat or chicken. There are a lot of goats in Accra. I did try the goat meat kebabs but found that they tended to give me a gippy tummy. I also found goat meat tough and too chewy for my liking.

In some locations you could order an omelette sandwich and could watch the omelette being prepared, placed between two doorstop sized chunks of bread and then fried to provide a just about manageable and very filling sandwich. Indomie (a noodle based food) was also available on the street. If you found a good cook and watched it being prepared, it was a great dish. Although freshly prepared indomie takes about ten to fifteen minutes to cook, it's well worth the wait. Whilst you're hovering you can almost taste the dish as you smell the onions, peppers, garlic, cumin, tomatoes, eggs, noodles of course, and any other herbs and spices which the particular street seller uses to give the dish its flavour. You were so hungry by the time it was served, you couldn't wait to eat and this invariably added to the enjoyment.

There would also be a range of fruit for sale on the street and in markets including, depending to a degree on the season, pineapple, bananas, mangoes and avocados. The sellers had an efficient way of cutting the pineapples and mangoes which looked so easy and maximised the amount of flesh from the fruit. Coconuts were widely available on the street, stacked up on barrows and were very cheap. You would be asked if you wanted one with hard or soft flesh. The seller would then tap the coconuts to check them, cut a hole in one using a huge lethal looking machete, allow you to drink the juice, (with a straw if you were lucky) and then he'd scoop out the flesh and bag it up for you to take away. I regularly drank coconut juice as we were advised by a doctor during our ICT that is was particularly good for any tummy upset as well as being nutritious and thirst-quenching. Then there would be the girls who'd walk by and in the road selling pre-packed bags of plantain chips (our equivalent of crisps but much better) from huge bowls balanced perfectly on their heads.

Sadly, certainly from my perspective, desserts are not particularly popular in Ghana, or at least that was my experience. I'm afraid I do have a sweet tooth and often craved something sugary. Ghana does produce its own brand of chocolate and amazingly, some substance used in its manufacture ensures that it doesn't melt so readily in the heat. It too is often sold on the street as well as in stores. I never found out what substance ensured its resistance to melting, but having sampled some, I have to confess a preference for Cadbury or Lindt.

There were, however, some sweetmeats which I grew to love and which were sold on the street in places which I soon mapped out and bought from regularly. My particular favourite was a ginger tasting paste, which was rolled into balls about the size of golf balls and which weren't to everyone's liking but I became a fan. My main supplier displayed her wares in a small glass case on a stall at the edge of the market at 37. More often than not, the person who made them wasn't there and another seller would step in and take my money and serve me on her behalf. It was a somewhat hit and miss event - whether the goods were there or not, but I was always pleased when they were. (Lizzie kindly bought me some of the sweetmeats if she passed 37 and they were for sale.)

Mobile street sellers are also common in Ghana. They either push a glass case around on wheels (a bit like a wheelbarrow) containing their goods or a cooler box to keep their produce cold. The glass cases would be full of spring rolls and rock cakes and the seller would hoot a horn to let you know they were in the area. The cooler boxes contained frozen orange juice and something called fan-ice. These were packets of frozen yogurt in strawberry, chocolate and vanilla flavours. I developed a taste for fan-ice which made for a cooling treat in the Ghanaian heat.

In terms of how food is eaten in Ghana, the right hand is the most commonly used implement to eat with and is universally accepted. Washing bowls and soap are always available when eating out or in to wash your right hand before and after eating. I have to admit there's quite a knack to gauging just how much stew and soup the fufu or banku will soak up to ensure you're not left with a lot of liquid at the end of your meal, but you soon pick up the art of judging. It's also quite normal and not considered ill-mannered to finish off your stew or soup by drinking from the bowl it was served in.

One of the more sociable aspects of eating in true Ghanaian style is the very literal sharing of food. There is something really communal and satisfying about sharing your food and eating from the same plate. I found this to be the case anyway. It is also completely acceptable and traditionally advised that there isn't the need to talk whilst eating as not speaking whilst eating is considered to, and probably does, aid digestion.

Of course Ghana, well Accra I suppose, has succumbed to the intrusion of the giant multinational food chains – I saw Kentucky fried chicken and Burger King places there. The city also boasts a range of restaurants catering for different cuisines including Thai, Italian and Indian. Generally speaking though, Ghanaians tend to be good meat eaters and don't appear to focus on cooking or eating vegetables as the mainstay of their diets. Every type of food was available in the largest supermarkets in Accra of which 'Koala' and 'Maxmart' were the best known and biggest. All types of food were available in these huge stores, but at a price. Unfortunately, my favourite products in the UK, which include all things 'dairy' and especially cheese and yogurt, were particularly expensive, as were many types of vegetables so, while I was there I tended mostly, but not always, to go without.

My experience of eating Ghanaian food is full of good and happy memories and I miss it. Fortunately, I never had a serious upset tummy whilst I was in Ghana although one was always advised to check out, if at all possible, how any street food you might partake in was being prepared. So, if you go to Ghana, enjoy the range of food the country has to offer, and hope that you meet someone as talented and generous as my friend and colleague, Awo.

A trip to Makola Market, Accra

There seemed to be no beginning and no end to Makola market, probably one of, if not the, biggest open market in Accra. It just appeared to go on and on and once engulfed somewhere in the centre, it was hard to imagine ever getting out. You were just bowled over by the vibrancy, colour, density and volume of people every which way you looked and moved. It felt quite claustrophobic at times and there was a feeling in the heat that you could hardly breathe as the masses of black people were moving goods on carts or on their heads, selling, bartering or buying every item you can imagine all around you. It was a buying and selling frenzy.

The vibrancy and colour of the place was intoxicating and the smells powerful. There were fragrant herbs and spices, the sweetness of shea butter, and often the fragrance of a woman freshly washed in the early morning as she brushed past you. There were also more pungent odours such as the freshly butchered flesh and blood of animals in the meat market and acrid dried fish mixed with the stale, earthy sweat of men, old and young, working to move goods in the heat of the day. It was a heady mix which was not always pleasant and which shifted as you meandered and inched your way from one area of the market to another.

What strikes you most is the apparent chaos, the mix of goods, volume of people and colour, although there were separate, if ill-signed sectors for major items such as meat, fish, vegetables, household goods and material to name but a few. Despite these unmarked boundaries between areas, the whole market appeared to be like an enormous jumble sale. Look one way and see an array of second hand shoes hanging in pairs on a stand, next to them, colourful patterned plastic shopping bags of varying sizes and on the floor, bowls of onions or cooking utensils. In another direction there were huge umbrellas dotted all around providing shade in the heat for the traders with their stock piled underneath.

Many of the stalls were makeshift although there were indoor areas within Makola market as well. One indoor area specialised in material and had shelf after shelf of fabric of every colour and pattern imaginable. Another section focused solely on material for funeral wear. The distinctive colours worn on these elaborate occasions were red and black but the black material came in an unbelievable array of different embossed patterns and textures.

The roads through the market were engulfed and full to bursting with lorries and vans unloading and loading goods in the streets with people wending their way around and between the vehicles. It was literally 'chock-a-block' as the expression goes. There were also women selling a variety of goods in the market from the bowls they balance so effortlessly and elegantly on their heads. Of these, 'pure' water is perhaps most commonly carried and sold in plastic sachets, selling for a meagre ten pesewas. (About 3p.)

I didn't venture to Makola market alone. I went with my friend Awo who undertook a monthly shop for herself and extended family. She had a long list with her and I didn't have to worry about getting lost so long as I could see her somewhere in front of me. It was impossible to walk side by side and, believe it or not, just keeping her in my sight could be quite a challenge given the density of people and the many distractions. She was very systematic and her organised approach to shopping seemed almost incongruous in the midst of the chaos of the marketplace. She knew the market like the back of her hand and bartered for all her purchases which would have been double the price had I been the buyer. She bought household goods first and once she had too much to manage, she chose a Kayayo to help her carry her goods.

Kayayo is the name given to the many thousands of girls and young women who migrate from the more challenging northern regions of Ghana (over 400 miles away) to find work as porters in the city markets. The journey they make is undertaken to escape an existence where subsistence farming is the norm and where living for them is synonymous with hard labour. They're lured south by perceptions of what the capital city has to offer but for many, it's simply a move from one kind of poverty to another and ultimately, for some, into a life of prostitution.

There are many Kayayo in Makola market who act as carriers for anyone willing to engage them. They wander around the market place balancing huge bowls sublimely on their heads, waiting to be picked for work. The bowls are balanced vertically, held in place with one hand, to show their availability for hire. Awo selected what she considered to be a strong Kayayo to help her. Although young, the girl was tall and strong and her English good. Awo offloaded her purchases into the girl's bowl which ended up being piled high with a huge packet of nappies on top. As Awo worked through her list, we eventually ended up with three Kayayo. I suppose it's a more personal approach than having a shopping trolley.

I was so moved by the sweat trickling down their faces as they patiently waited whilst Awo shopped that I took a photograph, after first securing their approval. We all meandered our way somewhat like a snake through the market place, Awo taking the lead followed by the three Kayayo and with me bringing up the rear, trying desperately not to lose sight of the last Kayayo in the line. Eventually Awo led our expedition back to her car and we off-loaded all her goods.

Ironically, given my focus on keeping up with Awo and the Kayayo and ensuring I didn't get lost in the melee of the market, I didn't buy a thing for myself but didn't feel a particular need to do so. For me, the trip to Makola market was an amazing and memorable experience which remains vivid in my mind. That is what I bought home and it didn't cost me anything. It was a place bursting with life, colour, sweat, heat and energy and oh so Ghanaian.

The Kayayo: A story with a happy ending

Awo felt that the first Kayayo she'd hired to carry her goods spoke good English and before we left Makola market, she questioned her about her situation. Her name was Memunatu. She spoke softly and smiled coyly when I asked her if I could take her photograph. She wore a long scarf tied around her head the ends of which fell, like pigtails, down the front of her. I wondered if the scarf was intended in some way to cushion her head from the weight of the bowl when it was full of purchases. She was tall and strong and seemed to have an inner confidence. As with many, she had left her family and school in the north of Ghana to seek a better way of life earning money as a porter in the markets of Accra. Awo gave Memunatu her mobile phone numbers and told her she could help her to return to her home in northern Ghana where she could continue her schooling. To my surprise, she did call Awo who made contact with NGOs in northern Ghana who could offer support. One of the NGOs was CamFed (Campaign for Female Education). Memunatu eventually contacted Awo to say she'd returned to her home in northern Ghana and had gone back to school which was great news.

The last I heard, Memunatu, who is a Muslim, had visited and stayed with Awo and her family over the Christmas period in 2013. I hope she continues with her education and achieves her full potential. Sadly, there are many Kayayo working in the markets in Accra who do not have the good fortune to secure a benefactor such as Awo.

Some Ghanaian customs and other useful bits of information

Ghanaians are friendly and mostly courteous, (except, in my experience, when the boarding of trotros is involved!). They place great emphasis on politeness, hospitality and formality. The Ghanaian word most commonly heard, particularly if you're an obroni, is '*Akwaaba*' which literally means *welcome*. A Ghanaian will usually speak when passing you and if you can learn a little Twi to respond, if only with a couple of words, it's well received. Although there are over 70 different local Ghanaian languages, Twi is the most commonly spoken and predominates in Accra. (A few basic Ghanaian words and phrases are included later in this section.)

Shaking hands and use of the right hand

Ghanaians always shake hands with the right hand. In fact it's impolite to do anything with your left hand in Ghana. Even pointing with this hand is taboo. The simple explanation for this is that the left hand is associated, traditionally, with being used to clean your bottom after going to the toilet. (In poor areas there would be no toilet paper.) The hand is washed afterwards but the association remains.

Ghanaians also have an interesting handshake. It takes a while to get the hang of it, but when you do it's good to hear the clicking sound it makes, just like you've clicked your fingers yourself using your thumb and third finger to emphasise a beat or rhythm. To do this 'special' handshake, first extend your right hand as if to shake hands with your partner. Grasp the hand and complete a traditional handshake - now the tricky bit - instead of releasing immediately, slide your palm backward slowly out of your partner's hand until your middle fingers are touching flat against each other; pause, then press the middle fingers together to create friction before pulling back and releasing, effectively using the other person's finger to snap yours. A successful handshake will result in an audible snap or click that will give you and your partner a sense of satisfaction and connection. The sound is, I understand, a reminder that you were together until you're reunited. Of course it's achieving the 'snap' with the middle fingers as you part hands which is the tricky bit!

This is a greeting mostly used amongst friends or informally. I was keen to practise this handshake and pleased when I got a good sounding click. Some patient Ghanaians would even let me practice it a couple of times until I got it right.

When meeting and shaking hands with a group of people, custom also has it that you shake hands first with the person on your right hand side, then work your way left in an anti-clockwise direction. This ensures that your palm makes contact with the palm of the person receiving the handshake – touching the back of the hand instead of the palm is considered insulting or unlucky.

Also, the right hand is always the hand you must eat with and use in any transaction, never the left, which, for the reasons already given, would be considered an insult.

Holding hands and hissing!

Homosexuality is unlawful in Ghana but, interestingly, it is quite common to see two males holding hands. In the west, this might be viewed as being at odds with the law but clearly there is an acceptance of the strong bond and kinship which exists between people of the same sex and of how this might be expressed in public. It was good to see friendships openly and warmly expressed through physical contact which was not viewed as indicative of sexual orientation.

In this respect, Ghanaians are tactile people and two girls or two men or even girls and boys who are not in a relationship or dating will hold hands, simply for friendship. Friendships and particularly family ties and bonds are strongly valued and kept in Ghana. There is much respect for elders and often women will refer to their friends as sisters. Whilst I didn't refer to my Ghanaian or VSO friends as 'sisters', I did feel quite envious of this strong sense of kinship and community. There is a real sense of responsibility for all family members and a desire to bond closely with trusted friends.

Polygamy is not unlawful in Ghana and so it is possible for a person to have many siblings and cousins. The elder sibling in a family has particular responsibilities for younger siblings and is expected to act as a role model within the family unit.

A custom I found quite irritating but which is common is that of hissing to get someone's attention. This is particularly used in a spot when trying to catch the attention of the woman or often young girl serving drinks or food. I have never hissed at anyone to gain their attention and didn't try it. It's considered quite acceptable though and is common practice in Accra. From observation, I would say it's effective.

An odd custom

Another custom, well it's not really a custom but more just *how it is* in Ghana, is the practice of males urinating in the street. I have to admit it's not a practice I'd instinctively wish to support but as there are few public conveniences in Ghana, I suppose, needs must. What did, on occasion, disturb me was the way a few men appeared to feel the need to urinate in an overt manner, seemingly appearing to show off in the process. Fortunately, this was quite rare. Whatever I felt about the practice, urinating is not unlawful in Ghana and is common wherever you are. It is also the reason why many public buildings and walls have the words '*No urinating here*' written on them in an attempt to keep some places clean.

Tell it as it is

It is also worth noting that Ghanaians usually say it as it is. I remember a volunteer being a bit put out because a Ghanaian woman she was working with said that her arms were getting fatter. This is not considered an insult but simply saying it as it is seen. It's also worth noting in this particular context that being 'fat' or well-built is not the issue it is in the so-called developed world, and I found it refreshing to live in a culture which, traditionally, doesn't view skinny as best. Having said that, with the increasing use of Information Communication Technology (ICT) and access to skeletal images of celebrity western women and girls who are viewed as role models, it's highly likely that young people will aspire to look more like women in the 'developed' world in terms of body shape, dress and hairstyles. With regard to their physical and mental health, this is, in my opinion, a great pity.

Asking directions

When lost and seeking directions in Accra, I found Ghanaians to be extremely helpful, bending over backwards to get you to your destination. I have experienced Ghanaians literally walking with me to accompany me to where I was going, even if it was out of their way. Failing this they would find someone else to help if they were unable.

Ghanaians hardly ever use street names though so it's good to be aware of this when asking for directions. I learned that it's best to ask for a landmark. I once approached a policeman and asked for directions to the VSO office in Labone. I was near Danquah Circle at the time and thought I was on the right road but just wanted to know in which direction to walk. The policemen looked puzzled and sent me in the wrong direction!

Taking photos

There is a need to exercise caution when taking photos in Ghana. Whilst children love to have their photos taken and will be thrilled if you're able to show them to them afterwards, adults are not always so keen. This is understandable in any culture but there are particular sensitivities to be aware of in Ghana. Some Ghanaians may think that the photos will be used to show their country in a negative light in the west or others may have fears related to voodoo or witchcraft. Either way, it's advisable to respect privacy and not assume you can snap away at anyone at your leisure. (Remember my experience in Jamestown.) Also, I was reprimanded one day for taking a photo of a statue of three soldiers which had been erected outside the army housing compound called Burma Camp where Awo lived. Taking photos of public buildings, as in Kenya, is, I discovered, prohibited.

Dress

A custom I really like relates to the dress code for work. Friday is the day when many Ghanaians opt to wear traditional dress to work. As there are so many beautiful materials in such bold colours and patterns made in Ghana, it's a custom which I felt showed off the Ghanaian love for all things vibrant and cool. Ghanaian women do, however, tend to wear quite figure hugging long skirts and dresses.

I had a traditional outfit made for me but it took several fittings to get Betty, my talented dressmaker, to take out the seam in the skirt sufficiently to enable me to walk rather than shuffle around in it. '*I can't walk in this*,' was, I think, one of the first comments I made although it looked beautiful if I stood up straight, held my stomach in, didn't breathe and didn't move. We got there eventually, but sadly it was still too tight and too beautiful for me to wear on a trotro to work. I know I couldn't have got on a trotro wearing the skirt, not with any dignity anyway. So one Friday, I took it to work neatly folded in a bag and changed into it when I got there. I had photos ceremoniously taken in front of the White House where I worked and then changed back into my 'ordinary' clothes. The skirt and top, whilst looking beautiful, were too uncomfortable to wear in work. I just felt too constrained.

Hair and hairstyles

Many Ghanaian women, like women the world over, spend a lot of time looking after and grooming their hair. Culturally, braiding, which is also known as cornrows, rows or canerows is common and is a traditional African form of dressing hair. To achieve this style, the hair is braided very close to the scalp, using an underhand, upward motion to produce a continuous, raised row. Cornrows are often formed, as the name implies, in simple, straight lines, but they can also be formed in complicated geometric or curvilinear designs. Hair which is braided is popular because it's easy to maintain. The rows can be left for weeks at a time if looked after through careful washing of the hair and regular oiling of the scalp. Cornrowed hairstyles are sometimes decorated with beads. Although men and women may braid their hair, it was mostly done by women for women in Ghana.

Having said that, Waqas had his hair braided during his placement in Ghana. Katie did too. From a short, auburn bob her head of hair was transformed into nearly waist long auburn braids which looked amazing and lasted for weeks.

Many women in Ghana also choose to wear wigs or hair pieces and there are many many shops which stock them. It's a big industry. (Accra Mall had a shop which only sold wigs and hair pieces!)

Without wishing to go into the politics of black women's hair styles and choices, and the reasons many appear to aspire to a more Western look with long, sleek hair, what I would say is that braiding hair is a real art and can look amazing. I also think that black women who wear their natural hair short look equally beautiful and stunning. But I've no idea how women in Ghana get used to wearing a wig in the Ghanaian heat.

Ghanaian men are also well groomed and there are many barbers displaying the variety of styles which can be created for their hair type.

Funerals

It is advised in planning meetings at work that Fridays are days to be avoided due to the number of people who need to take them off to attend a funeral. These events tend to run all the way through from Friday to Sunday and include the provision of food, drink, music and the opportunity for dancing. They are often signposted in towns/communities to enable all family members, close and distant, and friends to attend. Traditional Ghanaian attire for funerals is black and red which is striking. I have seen some of the most beautiful black embossed material for funeral dresses (at Makola market). Maybe the colours are to strike a balance between the sombre and the happy – a reflection of sorrow for a loss and the celebration of a life. Ghana is also famous for making elaborate coffins for the dead which may be shaped to represent some element of the deceased including his or her occupation or passion. They can come in an array of elaborate shapes and sizes from beer bottles, fish, fruit, animals, aeroplanes to shoes.

Symbols

Ghana has many fascinating symbols (known as Adinkra) that originate from its ancestral history. Adinkra are visual symbols created in the past by the Akan people. The symbols represent popular proverbs, aphorisms, concepts and maxims.

Adinkra is also the name given to a cotton cloth produced in Ghana (and Cote d'Ivoire) which has traditional Akan symbols stamped upon it. As well as their use in fabrics, Adinkra are used extensively on pottery, logos and in advertising. They are also incorporated into walls and other architectural features.

The symbol on the first page inside this book is often seen throughout Ghana and means 'Except from God'. It is the symbol representing the supremacy of God. It is by far the most popular symbol used for decoration and reflects the deeply religious character of Ghanaian people.

Summary

There are many, many more Ghanaian customs and traditions related to the country's history, politics, values, Chiefdoms and communities but I hope the few I've mentioned give a flavour.

I think Ghanaians love ceremonials of all descriptions from christenings to weddings and funerals. These provide the opportunity for Ghanaians to dress up in traditional costume, dance to traditional music (usually played very loud!), eat traditional Ghanaian food and drink, which is offered in abundance, and, above all else, to socialise.

They love to party and are a gregarious race of people who are demonstrative, warm and gracious. They love people. I hope as the country continues to develop and modernise, it will not lose its wonderful culture, traditions and customs.

Some basic words and phrases in Twi:

How are you?
Wo ho to sen? (formal, or the shorter informal version which is *Ete sen?*)

And you?
Na wo nso ɛ?

I'm doing well.
Me ho ye (formal – literally *'my body is fine'*).

I'm fine.
Eye (informal).

Welcome.
Akwaaba.

What is the fare?
Wo bay jay sen?

How much is this?
Ne bo ye ahe?

Reduce it.
Te so kakra ma me.

A little bit, or small, small.
Kakra kakra.

Sorry.
Koo se.

What is your name?
Wo fre wo sen?

My name is…
Me dim de…

Where do you come from?
Wo fri he?

I come from England.
Me fi England.

Greetings

Good morning.
Maa kye.

Good afternoon.
Maaha.

Good evening.
Maadwo.

Good night.
Dayie.

Goodbye.
Nantew yie o.

Thank you.
Me da wo ase.

The greetings above are quite straightforward but the response to these depends on the age of the person greeting you which starts to get a bit tricky so I won't go into detail.

Ghanaians frequently add an 'o' to the end of a word or at the end of a sentence for informal emphasis, so Da yie would become Da yie o. I wondered if Twi for good night might be the origin of the well-known song: *'Da yie o, da yie o, daylight come and he won't go home'* but I never found out for sure. Use of the 'o' is generally confined to friends. I did learn a little more Twi but could always get by with a few simple greetings and of course my English, which is the official language in Ghana.

You may come across the name 'Charlie' quite often too. It's used informally as we might say the word buddy or mate. So the expression might be 'hey Charlie' or 'no Charlie', even if Charlie isn't your name!

There are other Ghanaian words which are useful to know. For example if you're asked to 'dash it to me', the word dash means to give it as a gift. The word might be used if you're bartering for something in the market or if someone simply sees something you have that they would like. A Ghanaian might also ask you to 'gift' something to them, which would mean the same as to dash them something. As a white person or Westerner living in Ghana, it's assumed by many that you are rich. In this respect, some people will think nothing of asking you for money or to gift them something that you have. Whilst we might think it rude and forward, Ghanaians wouldn't necessarily see it that way.

By God's Grace

Ghana is a country where the majority of people appear to actively and openly practice their religion and faith. Wikipedia claims that just over 70% of Ghanaians consider themselves to be Christian according to the 2010 census, with 17% of the population Muslim. Of the Christian population, 28% were recorded as Pentecostal/Charismatic, 18% Protestant and 13% Catholic. I'm not sure about the nuances between the different Christian religions; I just know that I felt a strong sense that Ghana was a deeply religious country.

There was a mix of religions in the capital city of Accra and religious tolerance was high. There were certainly enclaves where the majority of the population was Muslim, as evidenced by the traditional dress of the men and women and there were many Muslim elders sitting or lying at prayer or begging along the roadside adjacent to Nima, one of the poorest areas in Accra. I never walked through Nima but the trotros I took to the city centre drove through it. Everything in the area looked makeshift, impermanent, squalid, exuding poverty. There was rubbish everywhere, abandoned pieces of metal, wood, rubble, goats, dogs interspersed with wooden shacks selling food, offering different services and selling various goods. I don't think I would have felt too comfortable walking through parts of Nima alone although I'm sure I would have been fine.

The further north you travelled in Ghana, Islam appeared to predominate. This was certainly the case in Tamale which was the most northern city in Ghana that I visited. (See later.)

From where I lived, I could hear the call to prayer from the nearest local mosque (which I'd pass on a trotro to Shangri-la) early in the mornings and I could also hear gospel choirs singing their hearts out each Sunday. You could not miss the religious fervour. So in my experience, religion plays a high profile role in the lives of Ghanaians and all the people who I worked with at GNECC attended church on Sundays. In fact church attendance appeared to be the norm for most Ghanaians. It was also not unusual to see colleagues reading from the Bible or reading inspirational passages or listening to gospel music online during breaks in work. I also found some of the spiritual gospel music uplifting, even if it was sung in Twi. It has an energy and passion which is moving. Every meeting I attended whilst in Ghana, from Government-led workshops to local meetings or an Annual General Meeting (AGM), started, and was also likely to end with, a prayer. God would be asked to guide the meeting and those present to ensure positive outcomes.

It was also not uncommon to be on a trotro when someone would stand up or get onto the bus or even suddenly move to the front of the mini-bus and start preaching with gusto, quoting from the Bible. This happened to me on quite a few occasions. I didn't and don't go to church regularly but did go to a beautiful Catholic church a few times whilst I lived in

Ghana and I went on Christmas Day. The church was located in Airport West near to where Mungo lived. It was a modern, cavernous building, built of a light coloured stone and looked recently built. It had a magnificent stained glass window at the front, although two other large windows were just open holes. Clearly, resources had run out. There was, nevertheless, a wonderful sense of light, peace and calm in the church.

I'm not Catholic but I'd heard the choir rehearsing at the church as I walked past when I was taking Mungo out and it sounded wonderful. I just wanted to go in and see the choir singing and I particularly wanted to be a part of the ceremony and community on Christmas Day. The church was full, as I would imagine most churches were throughout Ghana. Attendance is not predominantly by the older generation either as young people are brought up to believe in God and attend church regularly.

Attendance at church is clearly a strong family tradition and an occasion when dressing up in colourful Ghanaian dress, your best clothes, is encouraged and expected. It is a joyous and uplifting event and I felt a true sense of community spirit within the church that I visited. Family life and filial responsibility remain strong in Ghana, supported by the church. Of the young Ghanaians that I knew, the elder siblings felt totally responsible for their younger brothers and sisters and considered it their duty to do all they could to ensure their wellbeing and career prospects. Young children also respect their elder brothers and sisters and show great respect for their elders.

Women (and men) are expected to marry in Ghana and as soon as they're married, they're expected to have children. It's what marriage is fundamentally viewed as being about. All these expectations seem to support more traditional family values which in turn are supported by religious beliefs. I had mixed feelings about this: I felt I wouldn't have liked the pressure to conform or being stigmatised for not marrying and adhering to traditional expectations of me as a female. On balance I would have to say I prefer the relative freedom we enjoy and general lack of pressure to marry and have children.

I did hear and read stories about more 'traditional' African practices whilst I lived in Ghana including stories relating to witchcraft and what is known as Ju-Ju. I didn't come across any examples of Ju-Ju in practice but believe it's still used by some, maybe in the more remote areas of northern Ghana. I also read about some villages who banish women who are considered to be witches. These are usually women who've never married or been able to have children. Being childless is, traditionally, considered a curse. Older women who aren't married and who don't have children are atypical in Ghana. There are, nevertheless, increasing numbers of educated women holding managerial and political positions and who are acting as positive role models for young girls. In the future, young women may hold different views on marriage and/or delay childbearing but culture, traditions and values can take a long time to change.

Religion still provides a frame of reference, a structure, a belief system, traditions, strong family bonds and Christian values for the majority in Ghana. So, as Betty, the lovely lady who used to do my sewing would say as you left her or in response to an event or anticipated activity: *'By God's grace'*. I think her response sums up the belief of the majority of Ghanaians.

Ghanaian children

In Ghana, babies and young children are most commonly carried on their mothers' backs, tied securely with a piece of cloth. This is called 'backing' your baby. I'd seen this in Kenya and it was something that interested me as the physical bond it created between mother and child looked so intimate and natural. I was keen to discover and try out exactly how they managed to do this. In Ghana, I was lucky enough to find out as, one day when I visited, Awo tied her youngest son, two year old Tetteh to me. I thought he might be reluctant, but he was fine. He was quite heavy and although he did feel secure, in a photo Awo took of me I noticed that I was stooping forward, clearly in an effort to ensure little Tetteh didn't fall off my back.

The method of tying the cloth to carry a young child is quite simple when you know how! First you pick up the toddler and swivel him or her gently around so that they are resting on your back, like giving them a piggy back. You take a long, broad piece of cloth and wrap it across the toddler's back, bringing each end of the piece of cloth round to the front of you, holding the child loosely in place on your back. You draw the top ends of the cloth forward and across your upper chest. First wrap the end in your right hand across your body to the left of your upper chest, and then the other end in your left hand across your body to the right of your upper chest and tuck these ends in tightly. You then pull the bottom ends of the cloth round to the front of you , making sure the cloth at the back rests under the toddler's bottom to hold them securely in place. You do a similar folding exercise, wrapping the end of the cloth in your right hand across your lower tummy to the left and the other to the right, and tuck them in tightly. This should hold the child firmly but comfortably in place on your back... in theory anyway!

I found Ghanaian children particularly appealing. You can't help but notice that they have the most beautiful big brown eyes and for some reason best known to our creator, Ghanaian boys are also blessed with stunningly long eyelashes. They are just beautiful and adorable.

Like all children, Ghanaian children love to play and those who lived within my local community could be seen most days playing outside. Dalali was about four years old and always shouted 'obroni' to me at the top of his voice. I rarely saw him without a football. Romeo was younger and quite shy but was protected and supported by his elder brother Elvis who was seven. Both boys were so polite and respectful.

I saw other children create makeshift board games, scratching out a chequered board on a stone path or wall and using bottle tops for counters. I would see children playing with old tyres, but none where I lived possessed a bike or any sophisticated toys. There were no iPads, tablets or music players, no dolls or action men, no magazines or books. The children I saw in my immediate Roman Ridge community had very little and yet always seemed happy. They made me think about the expectations of many Western children and the number of toys, games and electronic gadgets they have. Children from so called 'developed' countries seem to have so much, want and expect more, but are not necessarily happier or content.

It does make you think.

Aburi Botanical Gardens

I'd heard about the botanical gardens at Aburi but feedback on whether they were worth a visit was mixed; I decided to go.

The trotro journey was quite straightforward, requiring just one change at Madina, the small town famous for its market, a few kilometres north of Accra. As usual, the trotro filled quickly and we were soon on our way. It took about an hour and a half to reach the village of Aburi (about 35 km north of Accra). The journey was pleasant, taking us into highland areas which provided interesting new scenery where there are fewer houses and people and more trees. It just looked greener and more spacious with more air to breathe. The journey also afforded good views of Accra looking back where the sprawling mass of built-up Accra could be seen on a hazy skyline.

There was a small fee to enter Aburi gardens but, as I approached, I had a feeling it would be well worth the money and the visit. A map on a board just within the entrance outlined the different grid like zones within it. You could pay for a tour guide who would provide information about the origin, age and medicinal properties of most of the plants and trees – both native and imported, but I decided to go it alone and simply wander where the footpaths took me. Just *'going with the flow'* again.

Although the gardens were not like the gardens we might expect in the UK, as there were few flowers or flower beds, it was a place of great beauty and tranquillity. To me it oozed peace and calm away from the bustle of Accra. It was a safe and pleasant green lung and haven. The path leading from the entrance into the gardens was magnificent, lined by the most regal looking tall trees. (They're called Royal Palm trees and did provide an imposing entrance.) They dwarfed me with their long thin white trunks and sprouting fronds branching out like fans at the top. As a general rule of thumb, trees are so much taller in Ghana and really do look majestic. (That has reminded me of one volunteer who had a 'thing' about trees in Ghana. She waxed lyrical about the size and variety of them.)

My visit to Aburi was also memorable as it was the first time I'd actually seen a cocoa pod growing on a tree. I don't think the pods I saw were the most brilliant or abundant specimens as there were only a few of them. They were green, looked rough and leathery, and were about eight inches long with shallow ridges running along the length of them. Of course it's the beans inside the pod from which chocolate and other products are made. Each pod seemed to hang quite haphazardly from the trunk of the tree by a short brown stalk. I was surprised at how incongruous they look - almost as though they'd been put there by mistake and didn't really belong. But I took a couple of photos and was pleased to see what the famous cocoa plant actually looked like in the flesh.

There were also, I am reliably advised from subsequently studied reference material, '*many species of medicinal and economic plants reserved to be managed for the conservation of plant genetics.'*

Another interesting feature in the gardens was an old tree trunk in a clearing which had been used to create a piece of artwork. The tree was covered in figures and animals which had been carved into the trunk. These included a range of wild animals – giraffe, elephant, monkeys and human figures. You had to look quite closely to see all the different creatures but it was fascinating to study. It was a bit like a puzzle to see how many different carvings you could find. A further, somewhat incongruous, object which appeared to have simply landed or fallen from the sky and been abandoned in the garden was a helicopter. I've no idea where it came from and why it had been retained as there was no sign to explain its existence, but it was old, unused and, in gardening terms, had been left to 'go to seed'.

A further glance at reference material reveals that among the many exciting attractions within the garden are The Bush House, The Rock Garden, The Pergola or Lovers lane, The Ficus tree, and the school of horticulture. As I didn't have access to any reference material before I visited, I wasn't aware of these features as particular attractions although I'm sure I passed by or through them. When you visit though, you can check them out in more detail. I also discovered after my visit, that an array of 'personalities' (including royalty) have visited the gardens and left their mark by planting a tree or shrub there. A couple of notable visitors from the UK include Queen Elizabeth II, in 1961 and Prince

Charles, in 1977.

I really enjoyed my visit to Aburi Botanical Gardens. It felt as though its heyday had passed and many of the signs and descriptions of plants and trees looked weary and well worn, but somehow it didn't matter and felt in keeping. The history of the place was functional and to a large extent remains so. Tourists are welcome, but they take the gardens as they find them and appreciate the history, importance and innate beauty of the place for what it is.

For me, it was a place of peace and calm, somewhere to chill and take some time out for quiet reflection. We can all do with that from time to time.

Single, white female

Being single, white, and female in Ghana has its advantages and disadvantages. Maybe that's true the world over.

Ghana has a young population. The life expectancy at birth for Ghanaian women in 2013 was 62.08 years, probably indicative of the harsh life which the majority of women still experience in the northern and more rural parts of the country where they work on the land and are expected to do so from a young age. In comparison, the life expectancy at birth for a woman in the UK in 2013 was 82.80 years.

Culturally, as I've already mentioned, there are clear expectations of young men and women when it comes to family, responsibility, marriage and childbirth.

In the above context, single adult equates overtly with availability for marriage and white is synonymous, to most young male Ghanaians, with wealth. It therefore follows that a single white female generally attracts a fair amount of attention from Ghanaian men, whatever their age. Although it's legal to have more than one wife in Ghana, the practice does depend upon the material wealth of the husband and his ability to keep more than one wife. My view, based on limited research I have to say, was that the younger generation are moving more towards monogamy than polygamy.

So, despite being a 'mature' single white female in Ghana, it has to be said that Ghanaian men were generally interested to talk and to find out my marital status. In this regard, few questions were viewed by men as intrusive or too personal to ask, even when you were a complete stranger. I found taxi drivers were frequently the most inquisitive and, of course, they had a somewhat captive audience. It would be completely normal to be asked, firstly, if I was married and when I replied that I wasn't, the next question would be '*why*'. This would be followed by '*did I have any children*' and again '*why not*'. I suppose it would have been less complicated to say I was married, had a husband in the UK and four children!

The proposal

I was waiting for a trotro in late afternoon.

It was the equivalent of our 'rush hour': catching a trotro from the layby near the bus station at 37 was both chaotic and frustrating. There was no queue, just an amorphous mass waiting in the bus layby, all with the same intention of getting onto the next trotro. It might have been fairer if there had been a starter who shouted out, 'On your marks, get set and go', but I doubt if anyone would have waited under those conditions either.

So, unless I was prepared to elbow, push and shove my way through the mass of bodies which surged forward as a trotro approached, I knew I'd be stuck there for an age, watching trotros come and go until the crowd disappeared. I'd no idea how long that would take and so I decided to walk.

It was a long way to Shangri-la, the stop I would have got off at and, as I'd not walked from 37 to Shangri-la before, I wasn't sure how long it would take. But once I'd decided to walk, I sort of just kept going, even though it was hot and I was feeling quite tired in the late afternoon. Walking and actually making progress towards my intended destination was, I felt, somehow preferable to the waiting and the humiliation of not managing to secure a seat on a tro. It was so busy that the traffic on the Liberation Road dual carriageway was almost at a standstill, so there was also the added satisfaction of moving forward at a faster pace than the crawling vehicles. I'm sure I was actually going at a faster pace and even passed some of the trotros I'd failed to catch.

I was about half way along the route when a young Ghanaian male caught up with me and started to walk along side. I can't recall his opening line, but often, a man might ask to help with carrying whatever you had with you. I can't remember whether this was his opening gambit but he started up a conversation and it was difficult to be other than polite unless I was prepared to break into a jog to escape him or be completely ignorant and rude. He asked where I was from, which was a frequent and understandable question, what I was doing, about my family etc. and I politely asked some equally innocuous questions of him.

When we reached the point where I needed to cross the dual carriageway and go my own way to get to Roman Ridge, he popped the question. He just threw it into the conversation and asked me to marry him. I felt I had to decline, given the shortness of our courtship, and he seemed to take my refusal in good spirits. It's impossible to feel flattered by such gestures as they represent the desperate attempts of many young Ghanaian men to have what they believe would be the opportunity to leave their country for what they perceive as pastures new and greener. It's sad to think that Ghanaian men view the world in this way as the grass is not always greener and tying yourself, even if only on a temporary basis, to someone you don't know through marriage is certainly not the way to achieve happiness.

Whilst I can understand this desire and what fuels it, it's disheartening to think that young people don't feel they have the opportunity to thrive in their own country. For many who do leave, I'm sure they find that the grass is not as green as they perceive it to be.

African dance and drumming evening

A number of volunteers had joined a group to learn African dance and drumming on Monday nights and a performance had been planned somewhere in an area of Accra called Bubiashie. An energetic Australian volunteer, who was on a short, three month placement organised by another organisation (not VSO), had initiated the group and she'd managed to get some Ghanaian dance and drumming experts to take it.

I hadn't joined the group, not through lack of interest but mainly because I was really tired when I got back from work and the place where the group met was, in my opinion, too far to go after I got back to the flat. It would have meant getting showered, changed and then a further trotro journey to dance in the heat of the night. Half of me wanted to go but the winning half just wanted to stay in and chill locally, which is what I generally did. Samina went along to the dance group though. She was, as I've said, passionate about dancing. She would ask me each week if I intended to go and, despite my lethargy, was always encouraging. Fortunately for her, her journey to work was a mere ten minute walk away from the flat and so her energy levels were somewhat higher than mine when she returned from work each day.

The Australian woman, whose name escapes me, arranged to put on a dance performance one evening at which the group would show off what they'd learnt. I knew very little more about it other than the day and the name of the venue, which was a spot in Bubiashie. The group had Ghanaian costumes specially made for the performance. There were about seven or eight VSO volunteers who would be dancing. Sadly, Samina had arranged a trip back to the UK and was gutted she would miss the performance.

So I set off for the spot in Bubiashie alone and with limited knowledge about how to get there. It proved to be quite an adventure. I was fine getting on the first trotro to Circle (a major landmark/commercial hub in central Accra). There are several bus stations and markets at various junctions around the Circle roundabout. It's an area to watch your purse and pockets as it's buzzing at all times of the day and night and particularly crazy in rush hour in the morning. In fact you had to be cautious in most of the markets and bus stations as petty theft was common. Tudu, as I learned to my cost, was another area well known for petty criminals.

I knew I had to walk across Circle, which meant crossing dual carriageways, to get to a different bus station from where I'd been dropped off and so I asked a Ghanaian woman for directions to the trotro station to get to Bubiashie.

In typically helpful Ghanaian style, she actually walked with me through the crowds and took me to the bus station, checked where I had to be dropped off with the mate, and left me to take on the second leg of my journey. I was now travelling in unknown territory as I'd never been to this part of Accra before. I was told where to get off with instructions about where I had to walk next. It was dark and I was feeling unsure about where I was going. Stopping to ask again, another woman walked me further along the route to my ultimate destination, pointing to where I needed to walk before leaving me. Finally, a young girl asked me where I was going and actually walked with me to the spot. I was relieved to arrive.

Bubiashie is one of many unplanned neighbourhoods in Accra and so the roads were unmade and the area seemed poor. The spot was open air, as all spots tended to be, with tables dotted around under and around trees. All the volunteers were sitting at a table chilling before the start of the show. I was cheered and warmly welcomed for having made the journey. It had taken me nearly two hours. I'd already determined to get a taxi back!

The performance was late in starting, which was not unusual or a surprise. It proved to be the most exciting, action packed, fun and vibrant evening of entertainment I think I can ever remember. In addition to the volunteers, there were many other dancers and performers, which I hadn't expected, who were breath-taking in terms of their skill and daring. They combined hand stands, splits, high jumps, somersaults, body contortions you'd have to be double jointed to achieve, with rhythmic, pulsating dance. Many of the performers were accompanied by African drummers and the drummers also performed on their own as a group. They wore traditional, brightly coloured and patterned costumes and played on drums and congas as well as a range of percussion instruments. The sound of the drumming is intoxicating. It was hypnotic and highly charged. In African drumming, playing maintains a prolonged frenzy of rhythms with hands pounding the drums and shaking percussive instruments. All that was accompanied by singing, shouting and much laughter. There is something so primal about the intensity of the sounds and the incredible energy and complexity of the rhythms they produce. It is all mesmerizing... and very loud!

The evening was in fact packed with dancers and entertainers, mostly Ghanaian men performing in groups or in pairs. All had brilliant timing, co-ordination, rhythm, gyrating hips and bodies. Parts of the performances reminded me of a circus as the dancers were so acrobatic. One man even ate fire as part of his act. I was taken aback by the performance of one Ghanaian man who was severely disabled. He had no legs but his muscular body and shoulders enabled him to move with ease. His arms were strong and his hands expressive as he made the dance floor his own. It had the audience spell bound. I had never seen such a dramatic performing artist. It was powerful and at the same time un-nerving to see him moving rhythmically across the floor with no inhibitions. I suppose it shook my expectations of what someone with such profound disabilities could achieve. I felt out of my own comfort zone watching him use his shortened body to move so effortlessly in time to the music with such confidence and love of his art.

The dance the volunteers performed was great fun to watch. As the sole VSO volunteer not in on the act, I was charged with taking photos and snapped away quite happily although given the constant movement of the dancers, getting clear photos proved difficult. Sadly I also appeared to snap the rear ends of most of them due to the time delay in using the flash. One of the dances I'd heard much about was called the 'Cow dance'. I'm sure it had cultural and ritual significance but have to admit that it was lost on me. They danced their well-rehearsed performance with other Ghanaians in a circle in a very animated and gesticulating manner. Their costumes consisted of footless black leggings and a dress with a flared skirt and shoulder straps. All the dresses were made of the same material and design. The fabric was cobalt blue with a bold geometric pattern in red, yellow and orange. They'd been designed and handmade especially for the performance. I know they all had a memorable time, although I also know a couple of them were particularly relieved when it was over. As well as dancing, the Australian volunteer performed a solo on the drums as she'd particularly wanted to learn drumming too. She did an amazing job.

    The whole evening turned out to be a fantastic spectacle and a much bigger event than I think any of the volunteers, including me, had imagined it would be. It was an unmissable evening and most definitely worth the long journey it took to get there.

Scottish country dancing in Accra

If you'd asked me what, if any, form of dancing I'd be most likely do in Ghana, it would probably be salsa, traditional African dances or even Azonto, which was very popular at the time. (Azonto is a recent dance and music genre that originated in Ghana.) I'd never have said I'd be doing Scottish Country Dancing in Accra.

I, together with Cath, Kathy, Cat, Cindy, Doris, Desmond and Samina, all have Rachel to thank for introducing us to Scottish Country Dancing. We were all VSO volunteers or former volunteers, except for Cat and Doris who were consultants and Desmond who was Ghanaian. Rachel, who took over from Samina as the VSO rep for Accra, was Scottish and encouraged us. I'm not sure how she sussed out that this form of dancing was being practised in Accra. She probably made the discovery through checking out activities on the ex-pat website, I never asked her. The event was organised and run by the Caledonian Society of Ghana.

We'd meet every Wednesday night. The dancing was held in the Grasscutter's Return, a bar/restaurant within the recreational centre based at the British High Commission residential compound, Cantonments, in central Accra. It was a challenge to find on your initial visit, despite being given copious directions, but okay, more or less, after that.

For anyone who might contemplate going, there are directions at the end of this chapter…and good luck!

Rachel would ensure that our names were on the list at the entrance to the Commission compound as, for security, we all had to sign in.

To start, we'd order drinks at the bar and catch up with one another socially. There were usually a few other people at the event, but sometimes the volunteers would be the only group dancing. Then we'd be invited by the person leading the dancing to take to the floor with a partner. As there was a dearth of men, much like in the UK, one of us would elect to be the man and would usually be given a tie to wear for identification purposes.

The steps would be called out as we initially walked through the dance. After two or three goes, the music would start with the customary long accordion chord (the leader brought a cassette player and cassette with the dance music) and we'd do a few sets. The dances invariably involved linking arms, clapping, skipping, do si do, swinging our partners, ducking and diving (well weaving), creating arches and dancing under them, polka, and generally have fun. There were usually mistakes and mix-ups but a lot of laughter.

Cindy was particularly enthusiastic and really got into the spirit of the dancing, swinging her partner around and dancing with gusto. She had a great sense of fun, as did all of the volunteers.

I remember some of the dances which included 'Strip the Willow' and I'm sure we must have done the Gay Gordons and the Dashing White Sergeant along the way.

At the end of what was always a fun and energetic evening, we'd all leave together, sharing taxis home.

Directions

Grasscuttter's Return: (bar and restaurant of the recreation centre in the British High Commission residential compound).

Coming from Danquah Circle, going west on Ring Road, take the ramp on your right at Police Headquarters, up to Ako Adjei Interchange. Take the street on the right after the bus stop and before the interchange (Osu Avenue Ext.) The unmarked metal gate is about 100 yards on your left, right after Wellness Laboratories at the beginning of the turn. You have to park on the street. Tell security that you are going to Grasscutter's and give your name which must have been put on the list beforehand.

Accra art and craft centres

I came across the art and craft centre in Accra by chance while out and about in downtown Accra. I was with Pegi, my friend and volunteer from Canada. We'd shared a hotel room during my first week in Accra on ICT. Although based in Wa in the north west of Ghana, she was staying in Accra to meet up with her husband who was visiting her.

We were walking around fairly close to the hotel where she'd booked for them to stay when we came across the workshops and craft centre. The open-air workshops were scattered along a coastal stretch of open land, beyond which was the sea. The area was dotted with craftsmen stripped off to the waist in the heat of the day making drums and other instruments and carving statues. It was a makeshift area with wooden shacks and men working mostly under the shade of trees. There were children playing around and the general atmosphere was purposeful yet chilled.

I asked about the drums and was told that goatskin was best to use across the drum although I've forgotten why. I was then given an impromptu, personal drumming performance by three men. I asked about drumming lessons and would have liked to learn, but sadly I never got around to it.

Nearby was an indoor market where more crafts were sold. There were tightly packed stalls with Ghanaian cloth on shelves stacked too high to reach. Most of the material had vibrant colours and geometric patterns typical of the Ghanaian style. There were also stalls brimming with beaded necklaces, ear-rings and bracelets.

I found another craft centre which was off the beaten track but quite near to Accra Mall. I would visit quite often, mostly at the weekend and became well known to those who worked there. I would be invited to visit each of the many 'shop' areas (basically open, roughly built wooden sheds or shacks) which sold an array of traditional Ghanaian arts and crafts. It was impossible to pass each seller without being almost physically drawn in to look. It felt like an insult not to. The shops were packed so closely together with alleyways to the side often leading to more shops. There were simply layer after layer of shacks, alleyways and crafts. Each person's shop looked much like the other with bags, wooden animals and masks, paintings, dresses, beads and mirrors. Some of the masks looked authentic, others more modern. If you saw something you liked the best advice was to buy it then and there as it was difficult to back track and find the place where you'd seen it!

All the sellers were friendly, chatty and wanted your custom, even if it was only to spend a few cedis. It could also be tiring fending off the attention you would receive. 'Browsing' was a word few Ghanaians seemed to understand. Bartering was, however, the norm. I loved all the crafts and bought colourful bead bracelets to match the clothes I was wearing and some small wooden animals.

I also frequently passed and befriended another craftsman who worked with wood and who had a little wooden shack on the roadside on the route I regularly walked from 37 to my flat in Roman Ridge. I bought a few pairs of small carved heads of Kwame Nkrumah and his wife (about three inches tall) which he had made and three stunning wooden elephants. I've no idea how I got them back to the UK as they're all heavy and one of them in particular weighs an absolute ton, but I'm glad I did. They're beautiful rugged carvings and stand either side of the stove in my fireplace. He also carved a wooden bottle of Star for me.

Another craftsman I knew worked a loom in the open air not far from where I lived in Roman Ridge. He was incredibly skilled at weaving and worked so quickly. I couldn't believe how effortlessly and deftly he worked the loom, He produced beautiful woven bags, scarves and table runners in a variety of patterns and colours and could weave any message into the things he made. I asked him to make me a long runner with the words 'Stillness Speaks' running through it. To me it's simply a work of art which now adorns the full length of the top of my upright piano.

It was easy and a pleasure for me to spend many an hour wandering around craft markets watching such skilful local people making and selling their wares. As in Kenya, half the fun of buying in the markets was the process of bartering over the price. I like to think I became quite good at it, although I probably wasn't. As I've mentioned before, I'm definitely more willing to try my luck bartering in the shops in the UK now although shop assistants aren't half as much fun to negotiate with as the Ghanaians.

Alliance Francaise

The Alliance Francaise was both a school and a venue that hosted various cultural events throughout the year. Its prime educational function was to offer French language courses but it also had a bar where you could order snacks and an open-air amphitheatre which hosted a range of musical events and live performances. During my year in Ghana, I went to several events at the Alliance Francaise and enjoyed each and every one of them. The cost of tickets was also very reasonable being equivalent to about £5.00 in the UK.

I saw an amazing performance of Argentine tango and flamenco dancing by a woman whose feet moved so quickly it was almost impossible to follow them. She wore beautiful dresses which were skin tight over the body with flowing tails which swished around her as she spun and danced with staccato movement and flailing arms. She totally commanded the audience and the space on stage where she danced and stomped with tremendous energy and immense passion. For her final dances, she wore a stunning red dress with a long sweeping train and three layers of frills at the bottom. It swept the floor as she danced, her black hair tied up and back tightly in a chignon with a red floral comb in it to match her dress. She was breath-taking to watch.

She was accompanied on stage by a talented guitarist from Andalusia and two other men who mostly clapped the rhythms of the dances and shouted out (sang) loudly but not always in time, or, to me, in tune with the guitar but I'm sure that's how they were intended to sound. In fact some of it didn't always sound very melodic at all but it was certainly dramatic!

I watched Dela Botri, a world renowned flautist from Ghana at Alliance Francaise. He had a large band on stage to accompany him, all wearing the same bright orange patterned short sleeved shirts. They were like a big band and sounded a bit like the Cuban All Stars. There were also three female singers who sang with and danced to the band. Collectively they made a 'big' sound and had a huge stage presence.

One of the best evenings I spent there was to watch an all-African girl band called 'Acoustic Africa'. They were superb. The group consisted of three young African women accompanied by a male drummer and a man playing what looked like a huge wooden xylophone. The three women each had a distinctive style and role in the group: one wore a white sleeveless trouser suit and played bass guitar, another wore black baggy trousers, a fitted red top and wore her hair swept tightly and high on her head in a long pony tail which she swirled around. She played the conga drums with a vengeance. The third woman wore a long flowing red skirt which she flounced around as she twisted and turned and performed hip gyrating African dances. She also played maracas and guitar. Their music was eclectic African, rhythmic and at times frenetic. Their stage presence was hypnotic and powerful. At one point, the woman in the black trousers and the one in flowing skirt seemed to have a dance competition on stage, each trying to outperform the other with their head shaking, high jumping and foot stomping antics. The whole performance made your heart race and made you want to get up and dance. It was blood pumping stuff!

There was also a fantastic production from France at the Alliance which consisted of a series of short sketches. Each was unique, 'alternative' but brilliantly performed. Some were comic and others just out of the norm using tricks and unusual props. It was incredibly clever and included the use of mime and magic, creativity and imagination.

I also went to photographic exhibitions at the Alliance, a book reading by a number of female African authors who spoke about their books and life and art exhibitions. A bonus was that such exhibitions often included free food and wine. It was a great venue and my ability to visit made me feel very grateful to be based in Accra. The Alliance Francaise was an avant-garde sort of place and I felt fortunate that it was only about a twenty minute walk from where I lived in Roman Ridge.

Labardi Beach

Labardi Beach and Labardi Beach Hotel are near Teshie in the Greater Accra Region. They are amongst the busiest and most well known in Accra. The beach is renowned as being one of the most beautiful along Ghana's coast with golden sand and sociable beach scene. The beach is maintained by the local hotels and on holidays and weekends there are often performances of reggae, hiplife, cultural drumming and dancing.

Time Out says:

> '*Reggae DJs play on Wednesday night near an open bar that is stocked with local and imported beers. There are occasional live bands, as well as acrobats and other entertainment. The groups come from around Accra as well as from neighbouring countries. The standard is very high and you'll likely catch something that gets you moving. It draws a mix of international students, reggae lovers, rastafarians and the less pious 'rental dreads' looking to hook up with a foreigner or at least sell some Rasta-styled wares. A worthwhile trip if you are in town*'.

Although very popular, it took me some time before I visited the beach and then I only went once during the year I was there.

I had a completely mismatched image in my mind of the beach which was bizarrely based on the UK model and bore no resemblance to what I found. I imagined a long stretch of open beach and little else. Why I imagined a quiet beach in Accra which is so densely populated is, in hindsight, beyond me.

The trotro I took to Labardi left me with a fair walk to get to the beach and as I was walking to it along the pavement, a young Ghanaian started walking with me. I'm not sure where he was going but we ended up spending the whole afternoon together and, of course, exchanging mobile phone numbers although I never saw or spoke to him again.

My first surprise was that you had to pay to go onto Labardi beach. (The fee is charged unless you're staying at one of the hotels along the beach.) This was a new one on me. There was a long queue of people waiting to pay the entrance fee, but, as seemed to be expected of me, I paid for the two of us to go onto the beach. The second surprise was that the beach was packed. As far as the eye could see, it was covered by huge sunshades, beneath which were wooden tables and chairs with Ghanaians and obronis drinking and eating and just chilling in the sunshine. In and amongst, there were traders selling trinkets and food.

The beach itself was golden in colour and soft underfoot. There were palm trees flanking the beach and the glimpses of the sea you caught between the tables, sunshades and chairs revealed the roughness of the Gulf of Guinea. The waters are not the best for bathing and are known for their dangerous undercurrents, but despite this people were swimming or just paddling along the water's edge.

We found a vacant table and the ice cold bottle of Star I ordered went down well. It was entertaining simply to sit, chat, and take in the Labardi scene. We took a walk along the busy beach where others were walking and also riding. Instead of donkeys, Labardi beach has horse rides. For some reason horses seemed, at the time, somewhat incongruous and far less docile than donkeys.

My abiding memory of Labardi was the sheer volume of people enjoying the scene. This was where Ghanaians and obronis alike came to spend 'time out', to be with friends or to be alone (but mostly to be with friends) and simply to chill. I never got to a reggae night at Labardi, but heard of the late night (4.00am and later) fun to be had there.

The death of President John Atta Mills

Awo broke the news: the President had died. We were in the office and it happened just before I was due to fly back to the UK for a break in August 2012. Despite the fact that I'm not Ghanaian, I felt the weight and sadness of the country's loss.

Apparently the President felt ill and was taken to the military hospital at 37 where he passed away. It was devastating news which shook the country although John Atta Mills was known to have been in poor health for some time. Atta Mills was the first President to die in office in the history of Ghana and was respected worldwide. Liberia's President Ellen Johnson-Sirleaf extended her condolences to Ghanaians at the time and said that, '*On a personal level his moderation and integrity stood out.*'

US President Barack Obama also paid tribute praising Mr Atta Mills as a '*strong advocate for human rights and for the fair treatment of all Ghanaians*', according to a White House statement.

Under Atta Mills, the country began its exploration of oil and he was credited for expansion in other areas of the economy. He was also acknowledged for developments in education, health, agriculture, energy, rural development, governance and international relations.

Following the President's death, the Vice President, John Mahama was sworn in to office in accordance with the Constitution. I was surprised at the apparent lack of media coverage and hence scant knowledge back in the UK about such an important event in Britain's former colony.

Voting for a new president

Ghana has a two-party system, which means that there are two dominant political parties- the National Democratic Congress (NDC) and the New Patriotic Party (NPP), although there are 23 registered political parties on the list of the Electoral Commission of Ghana.

The NDC is a social democratic political party, founded by Jerry John Rawlings, who was Head of State of Ghana from 1981 to 1993 and the President of Ghana from 1993 to 2001. The NDC lost the presidency in the 2000 election, and it was not until the 2008 election that they regained it with candidate John Atta Mills. The NDC's party symbol is an umbrella with an eagle's head on top. The Party colours are red, white, green, and black.

The NPP is a liberal democratic and liberal conservative party. The party is centre-right. The NPP symbol is the African elephant and the NPP colours are red, white, and blue.

The representatives of the two major parties at the election were the former President, John Mahama, for the NDC and Nana Akufo-Addo for the NPP.

As voting day approached on December 7th 2012, you could feel the tension and anticipation grow as the election was hotly contested. There had been a long campaign throughout the country which included rallies and conferences with speeches and TV panel appearances of the leading contenders. Each put forward their views and proposed policies to address issues and continue the economic development of Ghana. The main policies related to the growing economy and education and opinions were fiercely divided as to who would deliver the best outcomes for the country.

Different communities in Accra visibly displayed the colours of their favourite candidate. These were apparent as you drove through different areas in Accra on a trotro where bunting would crisscross streets declaring the affiliation of the community. As a general observation and in my experience, Ghanaians are vitally interested in and love to talk politics. I would often hear men talking about their views as they sat and drank in local spots. Of course as volunteers, we were advised not to engage in any political activity or discussion and to remain neutral. It was not difficult to see why this advice was given.

The day before the election was memorable as tensions, hopes and expectations reached a peak. It was also notable for the long parades of buses and cars which I witnessed blocking traffic as they hooted and honked and shouted their way to final rallies in different parts of Accra. I was on a trotro at the time in the midst of the hullabaloo. It was in the afternoon and I was trying to get to Circle to visit a volunteer who'd fallen and broken her wrist a week or so before. She was due to fly back to the UK for treatment and I'd hoped to catch her before she left. I got caught up in the traffic as we approached 37. It was crazy busy and I was advised that it could take hours to reach Circle. That was the day there was a scare on the trotro I was travelling on, but that's another story (the next one!).

I eventually reached Circle, having changed trotro due to the smoke incident. It had taken about an hour. At Circle there were parades of floats, coaches, lorries and buses all carrying supporters. Circle was busier and more frenzied than usual, which in itself was hard to imagine. It was crazy and a little scary too. There was a cacophony of sound from people shouting and blowing horns and hooters from the windows of vehicles. There was also much flag waving as car after bus after float after bus after open lorry passed by, all full to the brim with passengers dressed in the colours of their favoured politician and making as much noise as they could. I'd never seen anything like it. The noise levels were ear-shatteringly high. There was a wild excitement about the place and it felt almost out of control. It was an unbelievable scene. Ghanaians clearly vocalised their freedom of expression and exuberance in a manner which bore little resemble to the general apathy exhibited during general elections in the UK.

The day of the elections was a national holiday to enable voters to vote. A curfew was placed on all volunteers who were advised to stay indoors throughout the day. All passed peacefully and the eventual results confirmed that John Mahama had been re-elected for the NDC gaining 50.7% of the votes. All was not straightforward, however, as an appeal was lodged by the main contender for the presidency, Nana Akufo-Addo. The legal investigation into alleged voting anomalies and fraud lasted for months after the initial announcement, but eventually, John Mahama was re-affirmed as, and is (at February 2014), the President of Ghana for a four year tenure in office.

Scare on a trotro

I was caught up in the parades on the day before the presidential election on my way to Circle to visit another volunteer who lived in Adabraka which was a walkable distance from Circle. Progress was painfully slow due to the density of traffic and the bright yellow trotro I was sitting in was hot and airless.

Gradually, smoke started to appear from the front of the tro. At first, given the generally dilapidated state of these vehicles, I don't think anyone panicked. However, the smoke grew thicker and all of a sudden, people at the front of the trotro nearest the door started to move. The slow movement escalated as panic struck and there was a rush to get off the bus. For a spilt second I thought it would catch fire and explode and I would be trapped. It was definitely feasible and in that split second I felt real fear. On a more humorous note, I have to say that I've never witnessed Ghanaians move quite as quickly as they did that day getting off the trotro.

In the end, all was well. Everyone managed to get off and stared from a safe distance at the smoking trotro which clearly wasn't going anywhere soon. The mate and others pushed the bus to the side of the road away from the passing traffic to stop the stationary and very sad looking yellow trotro holding up the parade. I think it probably overheated in the log jam of traffic. Thankfully no-one was harmed and I managed to catch another trotro to Circle.

Visit to Elmina and Cape Coast Castle

Our plan had been to go to Cape Coast and Elmina early on Saturday and return the next day. These places were popular tourist attractions which both have ancient castles directly linked to the colonial occupations of Ghana and the slave trade.

I knew the journey to Cape Coast would take over two hours so an early start would have been preferable, but despite my Ghanaian friend Kwame being late by a good hour (he wasn't the best time keeper) we decided to go anyway.

The trotro for Cape Coast left from the bustling Kaneshie market. It headed due west, and arrived in the late afternoon. In marked contrast to Accra, the place where we got off at Cape Coast was eerily quiet. The lack of people, traffic and noise made it feel as though the place was becalmed. We could see the beach and coastline where there was an abandoned fishing boat in a lagoon and randomly dotted palm trees which looked like giant windmills stuck in the sand for effect. It was a painter's paradise. We hadn't been dropped in the centre of the town and weren't sure where the castle was so, as we'd have limited time to look around it, we decided to get a taxi and carry on to Elmina. It meant travelling west for a further 12 kms. but we'd stay the night there and return to Cape Coast to explore the following day.

Given the lateness of our arrival, and not having booked anywhere to stay, our priority was to sort out some accommodation before it got dark, (remember it gets dark in Ghana around 6.00pm every night), although we did manage a brief wander around. The dirty whitewashed walls of Elmina castle with its turrets and terracotta coloured roofs marked it out against an overcast sky as we approached. It was built by the Portuguese in 1482 (about 155 years before Cape Coast Castle) facing the Atlantic Ocean on one side and with the Benya lagoon on the other. It was the first trading post built on the Gulf of Guinea and is one of the oldest European buildings on the continent still in one piece today. It apparently started out as a trading post mostly for gold as well as other goods, but along with Cape Coast Castle, Elmina had become a major trans-Atlantic slave hub by the seventeenth century. The slaves were held captive in the cells within the castle before being deported. On top of a hill directly opposite Elmina Castle, there's a building of a similar style which is the St Jago Fort. This was built by the Dutch, who later over-ruled the Portuguese. The fort was constructed to protect the Castle from raids by other colonial powers.

Elmina and Cape Coast are both fishing towns where men and boats go to sea on a daily basis returning with their catch to sell at the local market. Their base in Elmina is right outside the castle along the Benya lagoon where colourful traditional fishing boats, or pirogues, are moored, packed in like sardines. These wooden boats are painted in bright colours and many have flags, biblical quotes and wise sayings painted on them. During the day, the scene which is often depicted on posters and paintings for sale to tourists, is one of intense activity. Women dressed in colourful batiks and young men wait along the bridge which crosses the lagoon for the daily catch. The catch includes mahi-mahi, crabs and squid which is landed, divvied up and loaded into massive metal tubs. These are then carried majestically and skilfully to market on the heads of the men and women. Later in the day, fishermen's clothes which include their favourite football teams' shirts, are washed and hung out to dry on lines stretching across the boats ready for use the following day. Reams of green or blue fishing nets with floats attached would also be bundled haphazardly on the boats resting before the next day's catch.

The marketplace runs along the Benya lagoon together with carpenters' workshops making new pirogues. The carpenters live in shacks right behind their outdoor workshops. The whole scene reflects the vibrancy of Ghanaian life, colour, skill and energy.

As bad luck would have it, there was a funeral in Elmina that weekend. Apparently the person who died was a famous Ghanaian footballer so a large number of people were planning to attend. As a consequence, we struggled to find accommodation. Every hotel we approached was full. Doing things impromptu usually worked out okay in Ghana, but this trip looked as though it was going to prove the exception to the rule. The weather had turned grisly and the drizzle made it unpleasant; we didn't have our own transport and as the night wore on, we nearly decided to head back to Accra. But after a lengthy search, we eventually found somewhere to stay in a small, isolated guest house which was on the outskirts of Elmina.

The following day, we headed back to Cape Coast Castle.

Cape Coast Castle is one of about thirty "slave castles" or large commercial forts, built on the Gold Coast of West Africa by European traders. It's believed that, like Elmina, it was originally built as a small trading lodge which was later extended to become a fort. It was occupied by the Dutch, then the Swedes until it was captured by the British in 1664 and named Cape Coast Castle. It has the same grubby and tainted whitewashed walls and history as Elmina. Inside there is a maze of courtyards, stairs, windows, rooms, turrets, and dungeons with rows of now impotent and rusted cannons lining the tops of the walls and pointing lamely out to sea. There are also piles of cannonballs lying around, obsolete.

A guide took us around the castle providing a pen picture of the history of the slave-trade, explaining where the slaves came from and who brought them to this point. Many African Chiefs and Kings were themselves involved in trading, ordering raids and kidnapping, and arranged markets where the captured were sold. We went into the dungeons where the slaves were kept. They're dank, dark, and the air in them stale. You feel as though you can't breathe and just want to get out as soon as you can for fresh air. Walking around the castle, it was impossible not to feel the weight of the history of the place and to wonder what the sordid walls had witnessed. You could feel the suffering and hear the anguish of the prisoners, old and young, men, women and children, held captive within the thick stone walls. To say it's unsettling or sobering is a gross understatement. It's moving beyond words. In one cell, wreaths had been laid in memory of distant relatives who'd disappeared through the 'gate of no return' which we also saw. It's a small door that leads through the outer walls of the castle where slaves were lowered into boats (exactly like the *pirogues* used today), and then onto the big slaving ships further out at sea to be taken to the Americas and the Caribbean. Never to return.

There have been various stages in the renovation of Cape Coast Castle and models of these stages and plans are on display in one of the many rooms within it. The castle and dungeon was first restored in the 1920s by the British Public Works Department. Following Ghanaian independence in 1957, the castle became the responsibility of the Ghana Museums and Monuments Board. All the castles and forts in Ghana are included on the United Nations Educational, Scientific and Cultural Organisation (UNESCO) World Heritage List.

I was so moved by my visit to Cape Coast Castle that I wrote a poem about what is probably the most atmospheric place I have ever visited.

Cape Coast Castle - a poem

Visit this monument
where dark black, nigger history pervades the castle
on the promontory, as it stares out
across the ocean.

See the decaying cannons and their rusting shot
now lying, obsolete
along the weather-beaten, whitewashed walls.

Let the palm trees mesmerise you as they sway, nonchalantly
along the coast.

Watch the waves tumble, innocently, onto the sand
belying a sordid past,
feel the stillness and calm -
yet the peace and tranquillity beg reflection.
It is here where you will know the pain which
remains writ large on the dungeon walls,
the passing years unable to scrub them clean
or purge the truth.

Here, you will witness the dank walls
barely visible,
dripping with the blood of the past.
Here, hunger and degradation flow out to sea
along sanitation channels
carved in stone floors.

Listen and you will hear the cries of the past,
the screams of women and children,
the jangling chains of men
shackled for life.

Close your eyes and see the anguish, the torment of wretched souls
shipped from their roots
and lost for ever in harness.

Yes, visit the monument,
this place of dark black, nigger history.

Visit this place.

Trip to a workshop in Tamale

VSO was convening a management meeting in Tamale with Partners for its flagship project. The project was 'Tackling Education Needs Inclusively' or TENI which was receiving resources from the UK through Comic Relief.

As the project I was working on at GNECC was related to and funded through TENI, I was asked by the National Co-ordinator to attend with a colleague. This would be my first trip to the north of Ghana and I was pleased to have the opportunity to go. However I'd be flying rather than taking a bus which was a huge bonus. The bus trip would have taken about 14 hours. Flying took just over one!

It was touch and go until the last minute as to whether one of my GNECC colleagues and I would be allowed to attend the meeting as the flight was on Saturday, 10th December and there was still the potential for unrest following the presidential elections on the 7th. Fortunately, the okay was given and I flew to Tamale.

The landscape changed as we flew north. Trees and vegetation became sparser in the drier north and around Tamale it was decidedly more barren as we touched down in semi-arid savanna. The airport was small and all the taxis which were hovering in the airport car park were soon taken by passengers going into Tamale. It was only by chance that we got a lift from someone my colleague knew. It sometimes felt like everyone knew everyone in Ghana!

In Tamale, I had a spacious, air conditioned room with a king size bed, TV (although I couldn't get any channels on it) and a separate bathroom. I dearly wanted to have a bath, even if it was a cold one, but I remember there was no plug and I couldn't get one anywhere. I suppose it was considered a waste of water. It felt the height of luxury to stay in the hotel for a weekend.

The meeting/workshops were held over two days and it was particularly interesting to gain insights into the management of the TENI project and partnership working. I was keen to take the opportunity afforded by this work related visit to see more of Tamale and my colleague, who'd previously been a student in the town, took me around. It was very different to Accra. There was a distinctive smell in the air which was musky and earthy. It smelt as though pine joss sticks were being burnt.

We ventured into town after an afternoon workshop. The predominance of Muslims and motorbikes was striking. We walked around the market and my colleague helped me to buy two of the distinctive hand woven smock tops with symbolic designs that Ghanaian men in northern Ghana typically wear. I loved the market place. As in Accra, it was busy and colourful. We also went to a craft centre which sold a range of leather goods, carvings and beautiful rag rugs. I was tempted to buy one of the rugs but didn't. Something I regret. I would have loved to stay longer but our time was limited.

We flew back to Accra on my birthday.

Christmas and New Year 2012

The build up to Christmas was far less evident in Ghana compared to the UK. Sadly, in my opinion, the commercial hype in the UK seems to start earlier each year. We can see Christmas cards in shops now as early as October and adverts on the TV tempting children to start their Christmas lists start months before December.

I hadn't realised how much I would miss family and the UK at Christmas and I was sorely tempted to book a flight home. In fact I did reserve one and put a £50 deposit on a flight which would have left Accra on Christmas Eve. I didn't take it and spent Christmas in Airport West in Mungo's house. His owners were away and I'd been offered the opportunity to stay in the house with all its luxuries and swimming pool. An offer I felt I couldn't refuse. Most of the volunteers had booked to stay in one or other of the many resorts along the coast and I was invited and even provisionally booked too but didn't follow through.

I went to the Catholic church on Christmas day, even though I'm not a Catholic. The service was beautiful with traditional readings and carols. The highlight of my day was skyping with my family. It was special to see and talk to them all together but it also felt strange not to be with them.

Awo invited me to her home for a meal and to see in the New Year with her and her husband. I wasn't sure what event we would be going to in the evening. All I knew was that it was in Accra Sports arena.

It proved a memorable occasion to celebrate the New Year or what was called the 'Cross over'. It was a spiritual event attended by a stadium full of people. The programme included singing, (mostly in Twi), listening to speeches looking forward to the New Year, choirs and an orchestra. It was uplifting and moving and didn't finish until well past midnight.

It was not like any New Year celebrations I had ever experienced before.

Leaving Ghana

Leaving Ghana was hard. I didn't really want to go. I'd met so many people and felt established within GNECC. I'd also made strong links with the Special Needs team within the Government Education Service. I had work I wanted to continue and finish and felt frustrated that VSO couldn't support my continued placement.

One thing I did at the end of the placement in Ghana which I hadn't done in Kenya was to have a police check. This was recommended by VSO. It involved going down to the main police station in Accra, filling in forms and having your photograph taken. The police would then check their records to see if you'd been charged or prosecuted for any criminal offences during your stay and, I suppose, be considered an 'undesirable' should you ever wish to return. It took about two weeks to process the search after which time, if you had the all clear, you'd be given a paper certificate with your photo on it to confirm you hadn't been involved in any criminal activity during your time in the country.

I was lucky regarding the timing of my visit to the police station because, as you can imagine, there are loads of people who apply for these checks. I got to the station, located the right desk to check in at, filled in my forms etc. and as I was leaving, vividly recall passing a queue the whole length of a very long corridor waiting to be checked in at the reception desk. It could have been a nightmare wait had I arrived later, but '*by God's Grace*', I was spared.

I and colleagues didn't 'go out' to mark me leaving GNECC, but we did all congregate in the foyer area in the White House and had a take away meal together on my last day in work. GNECC's National Co-ordinator and all my colleagues said some lovely words about me, my time in the organisation and wished me well for the future. I expressed my thanks for all the experience I gained at GNECC and for being part of the organisation. It was emotional in a positive way. I did say that I'd return and kept that promise a year later.

I was also given some special leaving gifts which Awo had chosen for me. I received three Ghanaian dresses, a pair of beaded flip flops, three necklaces, ear-rings, a wooden pencil stand with tiny coloured beads on it and with the words 'thank you' engraved in it. I felt over-whelmed by the generosity and good wishes of my colleagues.

I was also surprised to be asked to call into the Government's Special Education Needs office before I left Ghana where I was given yet another leaving gift. It was a pair of Ghanaian style loose fitting trousers and matching top in Ghanaian fabric. Again, so generous.

I had a great evening at Afrikiko with all the volunteers and friends I knew to mark my departure from Ghana and appreciated everyone who came along and made it such a special night. I have many photos to remind me of that evening.

Awo drove me to the airport along with Kwame. As we were stationary in traffic nearing the airport, Awo bought me yet another gift from a young Ghanaian selling his wares along the dual carriageway. It's a wooden carving of a Ghanaian women backing a young child and carrying a water bottle on which is carved 'Akwaaba'. I didn't know how I'd get it back to the UK in and amongst all my bags but I did. It hangs on the door in my living room.

Return visit to Ghana, February 24th to March 24th 2014

Nothing stays the same.

I returned to Ghana for a month in March 2014. It was hotter than I remembered and I was ill with an infection twice during my relatively short stay and needed antibiotics on both occasions. This was in marked contrast to the relative good health I experienced during my yearlong placement. I stayed with Awo and her boys. She was a generous host providing not only for my accommodation but also wonderful Ghanaian food again. The quality of her cooking hadn't changed.

Awo had left GNECC in October 2013 and set up her own NGO called J.Initiative (JI) which she was focused on promoting and developing. I'm a member of the JI Board and am trying, where I can, to support the organisation to achieve its aims. We did some work together and I even stood in front of a large class of children attending a Saturday reading club that Awo was leading. I was amazed by some of the new words the children had learned during the week and brought to share with the class. I made the conscious decision that if I ever took this lesson again I'd make sure I had an English dictionary with me! All the children were eager to learn. I'd not taught for many years and confess that standing in front of a class of about 60 plus Ghanaian children was scary.

Awo ensured I was introduced to the other members of the JI Board whilst I was staying with her and I also spent time with a number of the Army wives that she is working with. (Awo is secretary to the Army Wives Association.) They were all incredibly generous and gracious. On one occasion I was taken by my Ghanaian friend, Kwame, to a resort with a swimming pool and open views over the countryside with the sea in the distance. I also enjoyed a pleasant afternoon just watching the sea and Ghanaian fishermen and women from a plush hotel bar located on the sea front.

I arranged to meet former VSO friends still based in Accra at the Grasscutter's Return where I relived my Scottish Country Dancing experience. Where better to meet up? It was lovely to catch up and to see everyone looking well. For an evening, it almost felt as if I'd never been away. I also returned to the VSO office in Lebone to say hello to staff there. Anita, who'd helped so much with all things practical related to my stay in Accra when I was living in Roman Ridge and arranged for the painting of our flat, had left the organisation.

A few volunteers I knew had finished their placements with VSO but had found alternative employment in Accra. Others had returned home or simply moved on.

I returned to Roman Ridge to catch up with my former flat mate Val who was still living there, but only just. He was looking forward to returning to the Philippines later in the year. He was the only VSO volunteer left in Ghana who was based in Accra. When I arrived in 2012, there were about fifteen of us. Before I left it was known that VSO's policy was to target volunteer involvement and placements in the north of Ghana rather than in Accra so as volunteers who'd been based in the capital left, they were not replaced.

I'd bought some colouring books and pencils for some of the young boys I knew in the community in Roman Ridge and met Romeo, Elvis and Dalali again. They'd grown, of course, although they remembered the obroni who used to live in their community and bizarrely befriended local dogs.

Some things, comfortingly, stay the same though and Betty was still sewing in one of the many small garage like workshops in the community and which we could see from the balcony of our flat. I'd spent quite a bit of time there being measured and trying on clothes she'd made for me. She hugged me and thanked me again for the clothes and shoes I'd left her when I returned to the UK.

I went back to GNECC and the White House. It was good to see my former colleagues and we talked about the projects the NGO is currently engaged in. I missed not feeling a part of the team, but it didn't seem the same without Awo's presence and it brought home to me how the organisation, and she, had moved on.

The dual carriageway which was under construction for the whole year that I was in Ghana, from American House to the White House, had been completed. What a difference it's made in terms of ease of movement and the appearance of the area. It looked such a chaotic mess during my placement when I struggled with the red dust on an almost daily basis as it was being built. Sometimes it was literally like walking through a desert dust storm. If we were lucky, the construction managers would arrange for water sprinklers to drive up and down the road to damp down the dust or it might rain in which case the whole road became a red quagmire.

I used to meander my way on foot each day of the week from American House to the White House sometimes gingerly walking a tightrope on partially laid curb stones but always amid huge diggers and machinery which I wouldn't have been allowed within a mile of back in the UK for health and safety reasons. There were no footpaths. This was Ghana. Most of us wondered if the Chinese who were managing the project, knew what they were doing. They clearly did and got there eventually. So things do move on and change is the name of the game.

I would like to think I'll visit Ghana again, but who knows. Whatever happens in the future, I hope to continue to maintain my links and friendships in the country which provided me with so many wonderful experiences.

Some dos and don'ts when you visit Ghana

So what are my personal 'dos and don'ts' for travellers, volunteers or anyone visiting Ghana?

Well, *GO,* is my first piece of advice. Travel is, for me, simply the best experience and really does broaden the mind. By this somewhat hackneyed phrase I mean it enriches you in many ways. You get to see places and meet people who, although fundamentally the same as you, are also different. They've had different life experiences and backgrounds through their cultural upbringing and they see the world differently. That's all good and makes you think, re-evaluate and is interesting to discover. Also, visiting other countries and taking in new scenery is a wonder and a privilege. The experiences are priceless and will stay with you all your life. So visit Ghana, but make sure you've got a visa and your yellow fever vaccination or you won't get into the country. Also check out online and read about the country before you go. There is a mass of information out there and it's all readily accessible.

What follows are a few of the dos and don'ts that come to mind from personal experience.

Remember, for starters, that Ghana's a tropical country so it'll be hot, and I mean *hot*, (average annual temperature of 26 degrees) all year round. Temperature does vary slightly with the seasons and elevation but it's still hot. It's cooler during the rainy season which lasts from April to July and from September to November. In the north, however, the rainy season begins in April and lasts until September.

Locals use sweat cloths (face cloths really) to mop the sweat from their faces as droplets of perspiration roll down everyone's face, not just those of the tourists. These are often sold cheaply by street sellers in trotro stations and markets. If you're out in the sun or cooped up on a trotro which will be full of people, you can't avoid sweating. So do be prepared for the heat and take appropriate clothes. I didn't realise I'd find it difficult to wear any top with sleeves and jeans or tight trousers were, for me, just unbearable. But young Ghanaian women seemed to be able to wear tight clothes including skinny jeans. Maybe they were just more used to the heat.

Ghanaians do have a strong dress sense and dress code though. If working in an office environment, professional, smart dress is expected. Most up market and professional offices will have air conditioning which makes a huge difference to the comfort or otherwise of the clothes you're wearing.

Health wise, remember to protect yourself at all times against the dreaded mosquito. You'll be advised to take anti-malarial prophylactic/medication which comes in two or three different forms or brands. The three most well-known are: Lariam, Doxycycline and Malarone. Check this requirement out thoroughly as new medications also become available. I know volunteers who caught malaria and it's to be avoided at all costs. It's particularly important as Ghana is high risk all over the country and the little buggers appear at dusk each night without fail. Remember also, that from personal experience, I can vouch for the fact that they can and do bite through clothes. I was bitten through my linen top even though it had sleeves and once got an egg sized lump on my back courtesy of a mosquito. So take the Deet with you and cover yourself with it thoroughly as well as taking anti-malarial mediation.

If you're staying in Ghana for several months, you may wish to check out taking a worming tablet too. (I thought they were only tablets for dogs or cats but not so!) Although not advised about taking a worming tablet either before my placement or during ICT, I discovered that many Ghanaians take one every few weeks. Rhys, Samina and I discussed taking one and decided to do so on 3rd June 2012. We each took one tablet called Vermox (500mg) as recommended by the pharmacist and lived to tell the tale!

There are plenty of pharmacists in Accra that sell a good range of products for minor ailments but they're more expensive than you'd pay for products in the UK. So take a selection of what you think you might need for tummy upset, bites/stings and headaches etc. Particularly remember to take some anti-histamine tablets in case you're bitten by the mozzies. The tablets help with the itching which can drive you mad (especially at night) and scratching can lead to infection. A good travel nurse will advise on this and all health-related issues.

Do remember that the pace of life is different in Ghana. Expect long queues in banks for example. 'Things' for want of a better word, do take a bit longer to get processed and sorted in Ghana. It's just the norm so if you have to visit a bank, take a book with you. Likewise if you unfortunately need to go to a clinic or hospital or, heaven forbid, a police station, appreciate that long queues are the norm and patience in abundance will be called for.

Check out the fascinating history of Ghana before you go. Visit Cape Coast Castle and Elmina and feel the history of the slave trade. Explore the many beautiful white, 'palm kissed' beaches (apologies for the tourist book language) along the Gulf of Guinea Coast and simply chill. Kokrobite was a popular beach destination with many volunteers and was within easy reach from Accra. Ko-Sa was another environmentally aware resort which was popular. It's managed by two Dutch couples and is located near Cape Coast, Elmina and Kakum National Park on the beach next to the small fishing village of Ampenyi. I also heard good reports about White Sands beach resort and spa.

Take care swimming in the sea though as there are strong undercurrents which, although I never experienced, I was advised about. If you want to swim safely, there are a number of hotels where you can pay to use their swimming pool without staying there. One such hotel, located near to 37 and not far from Kotoka airport is the 'Golden Tulip. I used the swimming pool at this hotel a couple of times and remember getting quite badly sun-burnt on one occasion. The pool was lovely and a good size for swimming. Also worth a visit is the five star Movenpick Ambassador Hotel which is about three miles away from the Golden Tulip. Although I never visited myself, other volunteers did and gave it excellent reviews.

If you love to dance Latin, seek out the many places where Ghanaians gather to dance. Coconut Grove has a salsa night every Wednesday as did Afrikiko on Liberation Road. You could spend a whole evening just watching the brilliant young male Ghanaians who love to dance and show off their skills. Salsa is a specialty and Azonto's cool.

For music lovers and those who enjoy the night life, Accra has much to offer. 'Chez Afrique' in East Legon is a great venue for live bands and good food and '+ 233' is a jazz club known as one of the best live music venues in Accra. The Labardi beach scene is renowned for its nightlife. Also recommended are 'The Lexington', the 'Republic' bar and grill and Epo's spot in Osu which has a rooftop terrace where you can order good simple dishes from the 'chop' bar next door. There are many, many more bars and nightclubs in Accra which are worth exploring if you have the time and inclination.

To fully appreciate Ghana, explore inland from Accra and visit the other regions. They offer a very different experience to that of Accra and each has its own traditions, crafts and unique culture. In one sense I'm saying do what I say and not what I did.

I didn't venture to the far north or west of Ghana on the buses and didn't see Mole National Park or visit Kakun park. Both are major tourist attractions. Mole is the largest and most frequently visited national park located on the grassland savanna in north west Ghana. Kakum park, a short distance inland between Accra and Takoradi, has Africa's only canopy walkway. It is suspended 100 feet above the ground and offers the walker a bird's eye view of the rainforest. From height, you can identify the colourful patterns of tropical birds as they glide through the forest below you (writing in tourist speak again!).

One of the reasons I didn't visit Mole was because I'd been fortunate enough to visit four national parks in Kenya including Masai Mara. I nearly visited Kakum Park the weekend I went to Cape Coast but time didn't allow on that trip. I know that the extreme northern and western parts of the country offer a very different experience to Accra and are worthy of exploration. The contrast between northern and southern Ghana is marked with much more basic facilities and poorer communities the further north you go. You just have to appreciate and be prepared for the fact that road travel can be quite demanding as some roads are poor and toilets, as we know them, non-existent. I'm sure road transport and travel inland will improve over the next five years though.

Do visit the Volta Region in the North East of Ghana which is lush and mountainous and be blown away by the scale of Lake Volta and the dam at Akasombo. The scenery is beautiful and the Wii falls stunning. You may even see black cobra on the walk to the falls!

Visit Aburi if you want to find some space a short trotro ride outside of Accra and to chill a while.

Learn a bit of Twi if you visit Ghana. (Twi is the most commonly spoken language in Accra.) Ghanaians will really appreciate the effort you've made to speak one of their many local languages and Ghanaians love to talk so be as open, friendly and warm as they are.

However, don't forget that Accra is a capital city and there are good people and rogues everywhere. Don't be a naïve traveller, watch out for thieves and keep your belongings in a safe personal place. Also beware of scams: I was caught out.

Remember that, for many Ghanaians, being white is synonymous with wealth. You probably are rich compared to most people who live in Accra. You will, therefore, be expected to be able to pay more if you stop a taxi or buy goods in the markets. So, unless you've got money to burn, haggle, and be prepared to do this. Don't accept the price of anything you are offered in the market at first. After a while you get good at it and it's what the local people do.

Don't get into a taxi until you've agreed a price for the fare (there are no meters in the taxis) and never accept the first price you're given. Look shocked and haggle. Also remember that many taxi drivers aren't like London cabbies. They might not know Accra well but won't give up on a passenger. If they don't know where you want to go, they'll phone a friend when you're in the taxi and they're driving along to find out. I've had some very long and circuitous taxi rides due to the lack of local knowledge of the driver. Also remember that Ghanaians tend not to use street names so you need to become savvy about local landmarks to get around. If you are white, expect to be hooted by passing taxis who can't understand why you're walking. As a rich obroni, you are invariably expected to take a taxi rather than use your legs. This gets to be a pain, but there's little you can do about it. Even if you can afford taxis, try travelling on a trotro. It's an experience you'll never forget!

Just to give you a heads-up when travelling by trotro or taxi, particularly if you have anything other than a crew cut, expect to be blown away, literally, as all the windows on trotros and taxis will be down and you won't be able to wind them up or slide them closed. They just won't budge! None of the taxis I travelled in had air conditioning and certainly most trotros don't have any. You'll arrive at your destination looking as though you've been dragged through a hedge backwards. I wore a head scarf for most of the time to protect my hair from the sun and also to keep it in place on trotros. It was whilst travelling on trotros that I most envied Ghanaian women, the majority of whom either wore a wig or had braids. Their hair remained immaculate.

Do try Ghanaian food - it is unique and spicy. Try street food too although be cautious and, if possible, the advice is to watch it being cooked. If you fancy a healthy and delicious alternative to Ghanaian food, visit the Sunshine Salad Bar in Osu where you'll be able to choose from an amazing variety of salads.

When in Osu, Global Mamas is a must place to shop for fair trade creative gifts to take home.

Do also try coconut juice which is widely available from street sellers. The seller will cut open a coconut, allow you to drink the juice and then scoop out the flesh of the fruit and give it to you in a little plastic bag. The juice is really refreshing and it's also nutritious and good for upset stomachs.

Think twice and be cautious about giving your phone number out to everyone who requests it. You'll invariably be asked for it by many people you come into contact with, especially if you're a woman. Think of your polite excuse and stick with it. Many Ghanaians would love to befriend you as Europe, the US, Canada and the UK are all seen as places of wealth, plenty and the lands of opportunity. Many, especially young Ghanaians, would love to visit and probably stay if they could. Getting a visa in Ghana is fraught and it's thought that obronis might help.

Remember that Ghana doesn't have a great deal of manufacturing and so foreign imported goods are expensive, as is any form of processed food. I longed for yogurt and cheese when I was in Accra. It is available, but it's expensive, as is chocolate although the local chocolate is definitely worth trying and I liked it. Remember you can buy most foods and items you can get in Europe in Accra, but they will just cost more.

Do check out the local crafts and markets. In Accra there are weavers and basket makers who produce amazing goods. I recommend this because I love all things craft related and enjoyed watching Ghanaians making a range of crafts from wood carving to weaving and making musical instruments, especially drums for which they're renowned.

Famous last words: do your homework before you go to Ghana and enjoy what will be a great and never to be forgotten experience. Use common sense, stay chilled and you'll bring home a raft of memories and stories, as I did, to last a lifetime.

Acknowledgements

Thanks go, in no particular order of priority, to all the members of the Bollington Library Writing group. Special thanks, however, to Nik Perring who leads the group and inspires us all, Jenny, Betty and Andy. I've appreciated the group's encouragement, support and comments throughout the writing and editing process. Thanks also to Anne, a good friend, for her support and input and special thanks to Debra Tracey-Carney, a local creative artist, for her cover design.

Thanks to all my friends and family in the UK who supported me whilst I was living in Accra and to Francesca who kept an eye on my house in Bollington while I was away.

Thanks to Awo for being such a supportive colleague and friend and to Kwame for giving me insights into Ghanaian life and culture from his perspective. And last but not least, my thanks go to: GNECC colleagues, Volunteers, VSO UK and Ghana and all the Ghanaian people who touched my life whilst I was living in Accra. You will all know who you are and I will never forget you.

Glossary

Accra – capital city of Ghana
Action Aid – A leading international charity supporting women and children in extreme poverty
Adinkra – visual symbols, originally created by the Akan, that represent concepts and aphorisms. Adinkra are used extensively in fabrics, pottery, logos and advertising
Airtel – a service provider for mobile phones
Adabraka – an inner city area in Accra
Airport West – an up-market area in Accra near the airport
Akwaaba – welcome
Azonto – a dance and music genre from Ghana
Banku – a food eaten in Ghana made with cooked fermented corn dough and cassava dough
Bubiashie – a poor, unplanned area in Accra
Cedi – Ghanaian currency (10 Pesewas to 1 cedi)
Chop – local Ghanaian Food
Charlie – term used to describe or greet a friend. Hey Charlie!
Circle – short for 'Kwame Nkrumah Circle', a huge roundabout and commercial hub in central Accra and perhaps one of the best known landmarks where there were several bus stations
Cross-over – New Year
Danquah Circle – a landmark roundabout in central Accra named after a prominent politician Dr Joseph Boakye Danquah
Dash – give something as a gift

Deet – not a Ghanaian word but the recommended ingredient in any effective anti-mosquito repellent
Fan-ice – frozen yogurt
Fu-fu – starch based food commonly eaten in Ghana
Harmattan – wind which blows from the north bringing dust from the Sahara
Jamestown – one of the oldest and most atmospheric areas on the coast in Accra famous for its colonial fort and lighthouse
Jollof – spicy rice
Ju-Ju – historically referred to traditional West African religions. A West African term pertaining to some form of magical power coming from an object
Kaneshie – an area in Accra with an extensive indoor and outdoor market
Kayayo – young women and girls, who work as porters, carrying heavy loads on their heads in the markets in Accra
Kotoka – Accra international airport
Kenkey – starch based food eaten in Ghana sold wrapped in palm leaves
Koala – upmarket supermarket
Lights out – power cut
Makola – area and large market in Accra
Mate – conductor on a trotro
Maxmart – supermarket
NGO – Non Government Organisation
Nima – a poor, unplanned area in Accra
Nollywood – a name for the popular Nigerian film industry
Obroni – the Akan (or more specifically, the Twi language) word for foreigner and literally means "a

person from beyond the horizon". It is often colloquially translated into "white person" or "white man"

Organisational Development – not a Ghanaian word – a deliberately planned, organisation-wide effort to increase an organisation's effectiveness and/or efficiency, and/or to enable the organisation to achieve its strategic goals

Osu – popular district in central Accra famous for restaurants, night life, banks, crafts and Sunshine Salad Bar

Oware – an African game that requires an oware board and 48 seeds

Planned and Unplanned neighbourhoods – most of Accra's 22 planned neighbourhoods were developed in the colonial era and are inhabited by rich Ghanaians and ex-patriates. (Examples of planned neighbourhoods in Accra include Roman Ridge and Airport West.) After WWII and the emphasis, post-independence, on the development of Accra, migration of job seekers to the capital city increased, leading to unplanned communities on the limits of Accra at that time. Over the years, the suburban areas were absorbed into the urban area of Accra creating contrasts between planned and unplanned settlements within the city. Unplanned neighbourhoods are characterised by poor road networks, poor drainage systems, and insufficient water and electricity services. (Examples of unplanned neighbourhoods in Accra include Nima and Bubiashie.)

Red red – spicy red beans

Roman Ridge – an upmarket planned area in Accra

near to the airport (Where I lived)
Shito – hot, spicy sauce
Spot – equivalent of UK pub. Usually in the open air
Star – locally brewed lager
Trotro – local privately owned mini-buses used for public transport (Matatu equivalent in Kenya)
Tudu – an area in downtown Accra having a large market and bus station
Twi – most common Ghanaian local language of which there are over 70 (Others include Ga, Akan and Ewe)
Vlisco – the Vlisco Group designs, produces and distributes fashion fabrics for the West and Central African market and African consumers in global metropolitan cities
VSO – Voluntary Service Overseas
Woodin – the first African brand offering a contemporary and wholly African fashion range
37 – trotro station and area at a major junction along Liberation Road between Kotoka Airport and Central Accra which has a Maxmart supermarket, military hospital, market and a small number of shops

Useful Websites

Voluntary Service Overseas: http://www.vso.org.uk/

J.Initiative: http://jinitiative.org/

Millennium Development Goals and beyond:
http://www.un.org/millenniumgoals/

UNESCO's website for the Education for All Global Monitoring Report:
http://www.unesco.org/en/efareport

Global Campaign for Education:
http://www.campaignforeducation.org/

The website of Ghana's expatriate community:
http://accraexpat.com/en/

Global Mamas: http://www.globalmamas.org

Caledonia Society of Ghana:
http://caledonianghana.com/

Ghanaian Adinkra Symbol SANKOFA
'return and get it'

Symbol of importance of learning from the past.